بسم الله الرحمن الرحيم

الحمد لله رب العالمين

والصلاة والسلام على خاتم الأنبياء والمرسلين

In the Name of Allah, Most Gracious, Most Merciful

Praise to Allah, Lord of the Universe.

May Peace and Prayers Be upon His

Final Prophet and Messenger.

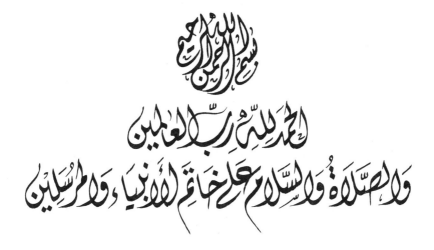

بسم الله الرحمن الرحيم

وَٱعْتَصِمُوا۟ بِحَبْلِ ٱللَّهِ جَمِيعًا وَلَا تَفَرَّقُوا۟ ۚ وَٱذْكُرُوا۟ نِعْمَتَ ٱللَّهِ عَلَيْكُمْ إِذْ كُنتُمْ أَعْدَآءً فَأَلَّفَ بَيْنَ قُلُوبِكُمْ فَأَصْبَحْتُم بِنِعْمَتِهِۦٓ إِخْوَٰنًا وَكُنتُمْ عَلَىٰ شَفَا حُفْرَةٍ مِّنَ ٱلنَّارِ فَأَنقَذَكُم مِّنْهَا ۗ كَذَٰلِكَ يُبَيِّنُ ٱللَّهُ لَكُمْ ءَايَٰتِهِۦ لَعَلَّكُمْ تَهْتَدُونَ (آل عمران: ١٠٣)

And hold fast, all together, unto the bond with God, and do not draw apart from one another. And remember the blessings which God has bestowed upon you: how, when you were enemies, He brought your hearts together, so that through His blessing, you became brethren; and how, when you were on the brink of a fiery abyss, He saved you from it. In this way, God makes clear His messages unto you, that you find guidance.

(Qur'an 3: 103)

إِنَّ ٱلَّذِينَ فَرَّقُوا۟ دِينَهُمْ وَكَانُوا۟ شِيَعًا لَّسْتَ مِنْهُمْ فِى شَىْءٍ ۚ إِنَّمَآ أَمْرُهُمْ إِلَى ٱللَّهِ ثُمَّ يُنَبِّئُهُم بِمَا كَانُوا۟ يَفْعَلُونَ (الأنعام: ١٥٩)

Verily, as for those who have broken the unity of their faith and have become sects—you have nothing to do with them. Their case rests with God and in time He will make them understand what they were doing.

(Qur'an 6: 159)

The Ethics of Disagreement in Islam

FIRST EDITION
(1414/1993)

The International Institute of Islamic Thought

Herndon -- Virginia -- The United States of America

1401AH—1981AC

The Ethics of Disagreement in Islam

Ṭāhā Jābir al 'Alwānī

Prepared from the original Arabic by
AbdulWahid Hamid

Edited by
A. S. al Shaikh-Ali

The International Institute of Islamic Thought
1414/1993

Issues in Islamic Thought No. (5)

Library of Congress Cataloging-in-Publication Data.

'Alwānī, Ṭāhā Jābir Fayyāḍ. 1935 (1354)–
[*Adab al Ikhtilāf fī al Islām.* English]
Ethics of Diagreement in Islam / by Ṭāhā Jābir al 'Alwānī; prepared from the original Arabic by Abdulwahid Hamid; edited by A.S. Al Shaikh-Ali.
p.176 cm.15 x 22½
(Issues in Islamic Thought No. 5)
Includes bibliographical references and indexes.
ISBN 1-56564-117-5 ISBN 1-56564-118-3 (pbk)
1. Islamic law–History–Religious tolerence Islam. I. Title.
LAW [Islam 7 Alwani 1992]
340.5-20 92-39110
CIP

Printed in the United States of America
by: International Graphics
4411–14th Street
Brentwood, Maryland 20722 U.S.A.
Tel: (301) 779-7774 Fax: (301) 779-0570

TABLE OF CONTENTS

NOTE ON ARABIC TERMS

In this English version of *Adab al Ikhtilāf fī al Islām*, it has been considered necessary to retain several Arabic terms because they contain shades of meaning for which there are no single corresponding equivalent in English. The term *adab*, for example, although it is translated in the title as 'ethics', contains the idea of standard norms and also connotes discipline, proper etiquette, manners, and training. *Adab* refers in general to the discipline that comes from recognizing one's proper place in relation to one's self, members of the family and others in the community and society. It also refers to the proper etiquette or manner of carrying out particular actions; for example, we speak of the *adab* of greeting, of eating, of reading the Qur'ān, or of dealing with differences of opinion. Loss of *adab* implies loss of proper behavior and discipline and a failure to act with justice.

Where English terminology seems in any way inappropriate or where there is a need to draw attention to a technical expression, the original Arabic is also included in the text.

The attempt is made whenever possible to explain Arabic terms when they first occur in the text. For easy reference, a Glossary of Arabic Terms is given at the end of the book. Arabic terms retained are italicized, except for those which have already entered American/English dictionaries such as: Allah, ḥadīth, ijtihād, ṣalāh, Sunnah, Ummah etc.

For Qur'ānic references the number of the *ṣūrah* (chapter) is first given followed by the *āyah's* (verse) number, for example (8: 46).

In quotations, brackets ( ) are used when a meaning of a previous word or phrase is given. Furthermore, square brackets [ ] indicate additional wording to clarify the meaning.

PREFACE

The publication program of the IIIT has already addressed important issues in the field of Islamic thought and the Islamization of knowledge. In this respect a number of books and booklets have already appeared in several languages under eleven main series: *Dissertations; Human Development; Indices; Islamic Methodology; Islamization of Culture; Islamization of Knowledge; Issues in Islamic Thought; Lectures; Perspectives on Islamic Thought; Research Monographs; and Studies in the Islamization of Knowledge.*

At the heart of this publication program is a deep awareness of the close relationship between useful knowledge and desirable social change. It is hoped that this book will be seen as strengthening this connection.

This volume is based on the third edition of Dr. Ṭāhā Jābir al 'Alwānī's *Adab al Ikhtilāf fī al Islām* which was first published in Qatar in 1986 and then by the International Institute of Islamic Thought in 1987 as a part of its *Islamization of Culture Series.*

The English version of *Adab al Ikhtilāf fī al Islām* has been prepared by AbdulWahid Hamid from the original Arabic. The number of chapters has been increased from six to ten by turning the author's original preface into the first chapter, dividing the second chapter of the Aracic version into three chapters, and making the conclusion into a final chapter. Some chapters have been edited to a certain extent, but the attempt has been made by and large to remain close to the orginal.

The author, Dr. al 'Alwānī, regards this work as an essential element in the treatement of a grievous and widespread malady that is presently besetting the Muslim world. Indeed, this is the disease of discord and division that has arisen from a faulty understanding of the meaning of the ethical guidelines prescribed by Islam for its conduct.

In *The Ethics of Disagreement in Islam* Dr. al 'Alwānī sheds light on the positive aspects of disagreement and shows how the early generations of Muslims put it to use as a fecund and vitalizing facet of their society. In order to fashion a viable Muslim civilization, argues Dr. al

ʿAlwānī, Muslims must relearn the art and etiquette of agreeing to disagree and thus become more capable of dealing with potentially divisive situations and issues. More importantly, however, they must master the methods of making disagreement work for them, rather than against them.

The Ethics of Disagreement in Islam comes at a time of acute and painful divisions and conflicts in the Muslim world. It is hoped that it will contribute in some measure to a raising of consciousness of the paramount need for Muslim unity and solidarity.

International Institute of Islamic Thought
Herndon, Virginia, U.S.A.
Muḥarram 1414/July 1993

Introduction to the English Edition

When the original Arabic manuscript for this book was under preparation over ten years ago, we never imagined that it would be perceived as an explanation of the etiquette envisioned by Islam for those engaged in discourse and disagreement, regardless of the subject. Likewise, the group we had in mind when we wrote the book was not the entire Ummah, but rather a small section within it.

The circumstances that led us to write on this subject were that a number of Islamic groups in the Muslim world had split up after coming under government pressure. Thereafter, they began to take opposing positions and soon fragmented themselves into numerous Islamic parties, associations, factions and coalitions, each with its own agenda. To make matters worse, the focus of each new group seemed little more than an effort to outdo the others in the hope of capturing the support of the Muslim masses. Yet the masses were totally confused by these developments, for most sincere and simple Muslims had always supposed that their problems would be solved when the parties calling themselves Islamic came to power.

Imagine their disappointment when those parties split and began disputing among themselves over abstruse points of fiqh and theology, entirely forgetting the higher aims and purposes of the Ummah. In their efforts to support their claims to represent "true" Islam, some of these groups went so far as to label other Islamic parties as disbelievers, apostates and heretics. While engaging in this activity, however, they lost sight of the higher principles and purposes of the Shari'ah which provide Muslims with perspectives far vaster than those afforded by pedantic debate over points of law and procedure, or fine distinctions between conflicting theological arguments. Rather, experience has shown that long immersion in such futile debate often renders the mind incapable of comprehending real situations and making value judgements on changing circumstances.

Since the book was originally intended to address these opposing Islamic political parties in one particular part of the Muslim world, the author went to great lengths to give examples from classical Muslim historical experience. In particular, he analyzes instances of judicial disagreement between the early *fuqahā',* differences that were not allowed to go beyond the academic domain or to cause hard feelings among the debaters and dissenters alike. Certainly, the differences between those early scholars never led them to lose sight of the higher purposes of the Sharī'ah or their responsibilities to the Ummah at large.

Although this book may more appropriately be titled *The Ethics of Disagreement between the Classical Jurists*, it nonetheless serves as a useful introduction to the subject of disagreement in general. It also lays down for contemporary Muslims many commendable examples of forebearance and understanding on the part of some of the greatest personalities and scholars in Muslim history. In this lies the utility of this book. And it is the revival of this spirit that allows contemporary Muslims to look forward to the future with hope.

Dr. Ṭāhā Jābir al 'Alwānī

Chapter One

The Malaise of Discord

The contemporary Muslim world is afflicted by numerous diseases which have spread to almost every aspect of its being. Moral torpor and intellectual paralysis, subversion from within, subjugation from without, the absence of justice and fair dealing, exploitation and corruption, extremes of ignorance and disease, poverty and waste, dependence and insecurity, discord and internecine strife— the list is long and painful. The number and gravity of these afflictions are capable of wiping whole nations and peoples off the face of the earth, even though some may be well-endowed with wealth and resources.

Beset by such catastrophic afflictions, one wonders in fact how the universal community of believers —the Muslim Ummah— has survived. That this Ummah has been spared and continues to exist to this day must be due to the fact that it still holds the legacy of the Qur'an intact as well as the example of God's final messenger to mankind, may the peace and blessings of God be on him. It may also be due to the fact that there still exist some elements of righteousness in this community who continue to depend on God and genuinely seek His guidance and forgiveness. This we may infer from a Qur'anic verse which says that God did not choose to punish even a disbelieving people because the Prophet himself was among them and there remained the possibility that they might yet repent.[1]

Arguably, the most dangerous disease which now afflicts the Muslim Ummah is the disease of disagreement and discord. This disease has become all-pervasive and affects every area, town and society. Its appalling influence has penetrated into ideas and beliefs, morality and behavior, and ways of speaking and interacting. It has affected both short- and long-term goals and objectives. Like a dark specter, it finally envelops people's souls. It poisons the atmosphere and leaves hearts sterile and

1. The Qur'an, 8: 33.

desolate. Multitudes of people are left contending with one another, and the impression is given that all the Islamic teachings, commands, and prohibitions at the disposal of the Ummah are there only to spur people on to discord and make them revel in internecine strife.

This is a trend which is in total contrast to the teachings of the Qur'an and the Sunnah.[2] After stressing the paramount duty of affirming the oneness of God (*tawḥīd*), both the Qur'an and the Sunnah stress one thing above all: the unity of the Muslim Ummah. Their object is to treat and rid the Ummah of any disagreements which disturb the peace and harmony in Muslim relationships and ruin the brotherhood of believers. It may also be true to say that after the abomination of associating others in worship with God there is nothing more repugnant to the teachings of Islam than discord in the Muslim community. The commands of God and His Prophet are abundantly clear in calling for the unity and solidarity of Muslims, reconciling their hearts, and marshaling their efforts in a single cause.

Since the Muslims have pure faith in and worship God alone, since their Prophet, their scripture, the direction they turn in ṣalāh[3] and the acknowledged reason for their existence are all one and the same, it must follow that they should be united in a common endeavor: "This, your community," says God in the Qur'an, "is a single community and I am your Lord and Sustainer; therefore worship Me" (21: 92). In spite of this, Muslims have unfortunately forsaken the uncompromising belief in and worship of God alone and abandoned the call to join forces with one another.

We need to be fully conscious of the dangers of this situation and make sincere attempts to deal with the roots of the crisis of Muslim disunity. To begin with, we need to restore "the dimension of faith" in the hearts of Muslims. This dimension has almost ceased to be the primary factor in regulating Muslim relationships. This is the result of a distorted understanding of Islam, harmful practices, and the pressures and impositions of non-Islamic societies. The restoration of the faith dimension and a sound understanding of Islam are the only true guarantees for rectifying our relationships, getting rid of our differences, and removing all traces of rancor from our hearts. How comforting and how

---

2. Sunnah literally means "path." It refers to the example of Prophet Muḥammad which consists of all that he said, did, approved of, or condemned.

3. Ṣalāh refers to the special act of worship or prayer performed in the manner taught by the Prophet.

delightful this would be! A sound knowledge and understanding of Islam would give us a proper appreciation of the various categories of actions: what is recommended or permissible, what is compulsory or obligatory, and so on. We would be able to keep before us the higher objectives of our striving and be wary of constant jostling with one another via argumentation and discord. We have undoubtedly lost the ethics and norms of proper Islamic behavior and the proper regard for moral imperatives and have thus fallen an easy prey to internal disintegration and internecine strife. This is the legacy of what the Qur'an calls "a narrow and constricted existence" and a life of failure. We have ended up in impotence and ruin. Such indeed was the warning of God: "And do not dispute with one another lest you fail and your moral strength desert you" (8: 46).

The Qur'an relates to us the history of the followers of earlier prophets that we may derive lessons and warnings from them. It shows clearly how nations rise, how civilizations are built, and how they flourish. It also shows how they decline. We are warned that decline and downfall are direct consequences of disunity and the disease of discord and sliding into narrow factionalism:

> And be not among those who ascribe divinity to any but Allah, [or] among those who have broken the unity of their faith and have become sects, each group delighting in what they themselves believe and follow (30: 31–2).

Disputes which lead to division and disunity are tantamount to abandoning the guidance of the Prophet and becoming alienated from him. God addresses the Prophet Muḥammad in the Qur'an with regard to "those who have broken the unity of their faith and have become sects" and says: "You have nothing to do with them" (6: 159). This verse expresses a condemnation of all sectarianism arising out of people's intolerant, mutually-exclusive claims to being "the only true exponents" of divine teachings.

This verse is applicable to followers of revelation which predated the Qur'an; their problem was not that they had too little knowledge or that their knowledge was misleading; their undoing was that they used that knowledge to commit injustice and sow mutual antagonisms: "The followers of earlier revelation differed among themselves only after knowledge had come to them, out of mutual jealousy" (3: 19). In the light of this verse we may well ask if Muslims are really the proper custodians of the last authentic divine revelation and the true knowledge and guidance it contains, or whether they are inheritors of the weaknesses of these followers of earlier revelation, their tendency to mutual jealousy and hatred, and the other patterns of destructive behavior they have set.

Disagreement, mutual jealousy, and religious schism were thus the factors which contributed directly to the undoing of the Jews and the Christians in pre-Qur'anic times and the superseding of their religions. Their history is a clear and permanent lesson for those who hold the legacy of authentic scripture (the Qur'an) and Muḥammad's prophethood. This fact is made more poignant if it is realized that there will be no replacement and no abrogation of the Qur'an. In one sense, however, this fact does provide some optimism that the diseases with which the Muslim Ummah is now afflicted are not terminal. They may either continue to fester with the Ummah persisting in a state of feebleness, or they may be cured. This is the outcome which many yearn for. Should it come to pass, the internal disintegration will cease and the Ummah will be back on the right course, healthy and full of vitality. These are possibilities which the final divine message holds out, and this is the responsibility and the challenge which it places on the Muslim Ummah.

How do we achieve this outcome? We should first recognize that there are natural differences in the way different people view things and conduct their affairs. There is an inherent uniqueness in each individual which contributes in large measure to the diversity which is essential for the building of human society. It would be impossible to establish social relations between people who are all alike and who have the same capacities. There would then be no scope for interaction, for giving, and for improvement. Diversity in talents and skills stem from diversity in individual mental and functional skills. When these inherent and acquired differences combine they make for human betterment. In all this we see the manifestation of God's power and wisdom.

If differences of opinion operate in a healthy framework they could enrich the Muslim mind and stimulate intellectual development. They could help to expand perspectives and make us look at problems and issues in their wider and deeper ramifications, and with greater precision and thoroughness. Sadly, with the waning of the Ummah, this is not the case. All of the positive advantages that can stem from healthy differences have given way to the chronic disease and deadly poison of discord which is weakening and eroding our spirits and putting us on a self-destruct course. The situation has reached such a state that some of those who hold divergent positions actually engage in physical annihilation while others take to regarding the enemies of Islam as closer to them than their fellow Muslims who share the same basic beliefs. Recent and earlier Muslim history has witnessed many sad and painful scenes when the vast energies and resources of the Ummah have fed and continue to feed the flames of discord, strife, and civil war which only seem to increase in intensity with each passing day.

Often people are unable to look at matters in a balanced, holistic way and see the various dimensions of an issue. Their narrow perspectives only allow them to see a minor aspect which is then inflated and blown up out of all proportion and given an importance to the exclusion of any other aspect or issue. This minor aspect is constantly commented upon and promoted. It becomes the basis for judging, disdaining, or accepting others. To strengthen this aspect, help from the enemies of the religion might even be sought against other Muslims who happen to have a divergent view.

It is related that Wāṣil ibn 'Aṭā'[4] was with a group of Muslims and they came upon some people whom they recognized as Khawārij. [5] Wāṣil's company was in a critical situation and faced possible annihilation at the hands of the Khawārij, who were of the opinion that Muslims who did not share their views should be killed. Wāṣil told his group that he would deal with the situation. The Khawārij came up to him and asked threateningly: "Who are you and your companions?" Wāṣil replied: "They are *mushrikūn* (those who associate others in worship with God) seeking protection so that they may listen to the word of God and know His laws." "We grant you protection," said the Khawārij and Wāṣil asked them to teach him. This they proceeded to do according to their own positions. At the end, Wāṣil said: "I and those who are with me accept [what you have taught us]." Thereupon the Khawārij said, "Go in company with one another for you are our brothers in faith." "That is not for you to say," replied Wāṣil as he recited the following verse of the Qur'an:

> And if any of the *mushrikūn* (those who ascribe divinity to any but God) seeks your protection, grant him protection, so that he might hear the word of God, and thereafter convey him to a place where he can feel secure (9: 6).

---

4. Wāṣil ibn 'Aṭā' is regarded as the founder of the Mu'tazilah tradition of thought. He died in Basrah in 131 AH. For more information on the Mu'tazilah, see chapter 5, note 10.

5. The Khawārij or Seceders. See also chapter 5, note 11.

"Allow us then to get to our place of security," continued Waṣil. The Khawārij looked at one another and said: "That you shall have." Waṣil and his group were allowed to go on their way and they all arrived at their homes safely.[6]

The anecdote shows how the severity of differences had reached a stage where the Muslim with a divergent view on minor issues had no alternative but to pretend to be a non-Muslim to escape terror and possible death at the hands of a dissident Muslim group who regarded itself as alone possessing the genuine, unadulterated truth. The non-Muslim enjoyed more security at the hands of these dissidents than a fellow Muslim!

Violent disagreement (*ikhtilāf*) and selfish, egotistic motivations (*hawā*) have a tendency to develop and grow larger and larger. They penetrate deep into a person's psyche and take hold of his mind, attitudes, and feelings. Eventually that person loses sight of the overall, total view of things. In the process he ignores the common, lofty goals and objectives of Islam and its basic principles. Such a person lacks vision and insight and forgets the elementary requirements of Islamic behavior. He loses all sense of balance and of priorities. Speech not based on knowledge comes easily to him, as do verdicts without enlightenment and practice without supporting evidence. With people like these around, accusations proliferate, people are branded as deviant and sinful, and others are declared unbelievers (*kuffār*; singular: *kāfir*).

A person afflicted with these shortcomings falls easy prey to blind fanaticism. His world is filled with darkness and gloom which in reality is but a reflection of his own miserable self on which the light of knowledge, wisdom, and prudence does not shine: "And whoever does not have light given by God, he truly has no light at all" (24: 40).

At the hands of blind followers and inexperienced folk, schools of jurisprudence and legal judgments and opinions arrived at by persons of insight and ability have degenerated into a sort of pseudo-intellectual factionalism and political fanaticism. Verses of the Qur'an and sayings of the Prophet are used selectively to support one position or another, and every verse or saying that does not agree with a stand of a particular faction is considered inapplicable or abrogated. The net result is that fanaticism increases and we are thrown back to the sort of ignorance which existed in pre-Qur'anic days when the prevailing dictum was: "The

---

6. Al Mubarrīd, *al Kāmil fī al Lughah wa al Adab*, 2/122.

liar of the tribe of Rabī'ah is better than the one who tells the truth from the tribe of Muḍar"–in other words, "My people, right or wrong."

The early Muslims did have disagreements. But theirs were differences of opinion and not reasons for estrangement and schism. They differed but they did not separate. This was because the unity of hearts and of objectives was far more important to them than selfish considerations. They managed to rid themselves of personal weaknesses and were keen to recognize and correct any lapses they committed. The Prophet, peace be on him, once told his companions about a man who was among the best of them and about the good news that he was of those destined for paradise. They examined the person's attitudes and conduct to understand the reason for his supreme achievement. The Prophet eventually told them that the person's achievement was due to the fact that he never went to sleep while there was a trace of rancor in his heart against any Muslim. The source of the calamity which afflicts us today is within us, in our hearts. Our tendencies towards isolationism are merely an expression of self-betrayal. In external aspects, we might not differ much from others. God says: "Keep away from all sin, open and secret" (6: 120).

On the level of the Ummah, we can look back and see that the Muslim world was once one state claiming its highest legitimacy from attachment to the Qur'an and the Sunnah. Now it has become some seventy-eight small states with innumerable and extensive disagreements among themselves. Each one of these states loudly professes unity, but in each state one finds several often conflicting entities as well as officially sponsored "Islamic" bodies. Often those working for the cause of Islam today who are ostensibly connected with the task of restoring the Ummah are not in reality in a better situation than the official organizations which they manage.

Our crisis is in fact an intellectual one, and it is very serious. When intellectual activity and output in the Muslim world is sound and when the Muslim Ummah once again derives its fundamental and highest legitimacy for its existence from attachment to the Qur'an and the Sunnah, it will then be able to uphold the message of Islam and build a civilization despite the hardships and severity of our material circumstances. We are assured in the Qur'an that "with every difficulty there is ease" (94: 5).

Our deviation from the Qur'an and the Sunnah has landed us in disputation and ruin, for God says: "Obey God and His Apostle. And do not dispute with one another lest you fail and your moral strength desert you." (8: 46). Islam put an end to petty groupings and internal

Arabia, each tribe or grouping had its own god to which it gave obeisance; Islam obliterated all these false gods.

Muslims as a whole today need not complain about scant material resources or about a straitened existence. They are in the midst of the consuming nations, whether of ideas or commodities for living. Their real malaise lies in the loss of the all-embracing significance of their faith and the consciousness of unified and common objectives. Also gone from them is the consciousness of a greater purpose and legitimacy in their lives. Paralysis has afflicted both their resolve and their decisive intellectual endeavor.

How do we get out of the intellectual paralysis which afflicts the Muslim mind and the moral crisis which affects Muslim behavior except by tackling the roots of this intellectual crisis and rectifying the methodology of thought? There must be a renewed stress on intellectual formation and the recovery of a sense of priorities. These goals must feature prominently in the training of new generations.

There is no way to achieve all this except by returning to the legacy of the early Muslims who were noted for their unswerving attachment to the Qur'an and the Sunnah. Part of this legacy was the unremitting search for true knowledge and the application of this knowledge. We need to recapture the spirit of this search and provide guarantees for ensuring that it continues. The link between knowledge and ethics must be restored. The principles and rules for inference and deduction to regulate independent reasoning also need to be put in place. Studies to ensure the unity of the Ummah must be developed, and areas of mutual cooperation defined with the object of achieving Muslim solidarity. All this must be done and pursued in a clear, systematic way through God's grace.

This book is a small attempt to chart the way ahead. Conscious of the profound tragedy which engulfs us, some have suggested that a book like this should deal with the objective situation now existing in the Muslim world and address itself to solutions for those contemporary differences and controversies which have made out of one Islamic movement in a single country ninety-three organizations independent from one another. Such a situation of course betrays the height of heedlessness to Islamic ideals and a morass of conflicting interests and tendencies.

One should, however, be wary of aggressive ignorance, the arrogant claims of fanatics, the troublesome and contentious nature of those who are obstinate, and the intrigue and plotting of conspirators. Refuting all of these tendencies head-on and clearly and frankly exposing the conflict ing positions and interests of the various Islamic groupings will not in my view bring about peace, calm, and cooperation in the Muslim arena. However, arming Muslims, in particular the youth, with a clear knowledge and perception of Islamic ethics and norms of behavior (*adab*) is a prerequisite and a guarantee for achieving such peace, harmony, and cooperation, God willing.

Knowledge of Islamic ethics and norms in dealing with differences, the consciousness of its principles on the part of various contending groups in the Ummah, and training Muslims to live according to these norms will undoubtedly release an abundance of energies in the Ummah—energies which are now dissipated and wasted in the theaters of futile internal conflicts.

When the Muslim mind becomes conscious of its civilizational role it will seek to win back those who belong to the Ummah but who are alienated. Conscious workers for Islam are responsible for the urgent task of building a sound and stable base for the restoration of the unity and health of the Ummah, and eventually for rebuilding the civilization of Islam. A single moment separates life and death. If our determination is sincere there is nothing that can prevent us from recovering Muslims from anti-Islamic influences for, according to the promise of God, a day will come when the believers will rejoice in the help of God and lost will be, then and there, all who tried to reduce to nothing the truth they failed to understand.

Chapter Two

The Spectrum of Disagreement

The Meaning and Nature of *Ikhtilāf*

The Arabic term *ikhtilāf* denotes taking a different position or course from that of another person either in opinion, utterance, or action. The related word *khilāf* is from the same root as *ikhtilāf* and is sometimes used synonymously with it. *Khilāf*, which basically means difference, disagreement, or even conflict is broader in meaning and implication than the concept of direct opposition. This is so because two opposites are necessarily different from each other whereas two things, ideas, or persons that differ are not necessarily opposed to or in conflict with each other.

Differences between people may begin with a difference of opinion over an issue. This may lead to argumentation and mutual wrangling and recrimination. The term *ikhtilāf* may therefore represent a mere difference of opinion or it could imply active controversy, discord, and schism. The Qur'an speaks of Christian sects that differed or were at variance with one another (19: 37), of people who held divergent views and positions (11: 118), of others whose beliefs and utterances were discordant (*mukhtalif*) in relation to the truth (51: 8), and of God's eventual judgment of people who differed among themselves and on the issues on which they differed (10: 93). *Ikhtilāf* may therefore refer to absolute difference in beliefs and principles, opinions or attitudes. It could also refer to situations or positions which people may adopt.

With regard to the discipline and history of Islamic jurisprudence, scholars have specialized in the study of differences among various schools of thought (*madhāhib*; singular: *madhhab*). One process by which differences have been perpetuated is for the followers of a particular leading scholar (*imam*; plural: *a'immah*) to stick to his deductions and rulings and disregard or put down all other variant or contradictory findings without giving any justification. Of course, if a person were able to argue and produce supporting textual evidence for his conclusions, he would indeed become a legal expert in his own right. On the other hand, a follower by definition is not one who delves into the details of juristic evidence. His only concern is to cling to the legal pronouncements of his *imam* whose authority is, for him, sufficient to establish the validity of any judgment or to counteract any divergent ruling.

Dialectics (*Jadal*)

The stubborn adherence to its own opinion or position on the part of one or both of two parties at variance with each other, the attempt to defend this position, to prevail on others to accept it or to hold it against them—these are all elements in disputation or dialectics (*jadal*). *Jadal* implies carrying out a discussion in a contentious manner in order to gain the upper hand. The term *jadal* is used in the sense of "braiding" a rope. It conveys the sense of stretching and arm-twisting exercised by disputants while each endeavors to force the other to accept his point of view.

As a discipline, the "science" of dialectics (*'ilm al jadal*) is based on advancing evidence to show which juristic rulings are more sound.[1] Some scholars also regard it as a discipline which enables a person to maintain any position however false it is, or indeed to demolish any position however true it is.[2] This latter definition implies that dialectics is not a science based on the advancing of any specific evidence, but rather a skill or a talent which enables a person to triumph over his opponent without ever having to refer to evidence from the Qur'an, the Sunnah, or any other source.

Dissension (*Shiqāq*)

Sometimes a dispute may become severe and harsh with the disputant's only concern being to get the better of his opponent. There is no concern for finding out the truth or for clarifying what is right. This precludes any form of mutual understanding or agreement. The term dissension (*shiqāq*) may be applied to such a situation. The word *shiqāq* in Arabic has the original meaning of carving out a piece of ground into distinct portions, and seems to suggest that one piece of ground is not wide enough to accommodate both disputants at the same time. Sharp

---

1 and 2. See *Miftāḥ al Sa'ādah*, 2/599, Dār al Kutub al Ḥadīthah, Egypt; also al Jurjānī, *al Ta'rīfāt*, 66, Aleppo.

differences from which discord and dissension follow place either party in a dispute in a "fissure" or a "breach" as it were, separate from that of the other. This imagery is implicit in the Qur'anic verses:

> If you fear that a breach (*shiqāq*) might occur between a [married] couple, appoint an arbiter from among his people and an arbiter from among her people (4: 35).
>
> And if others come to believe in the way you believe, they will indeed find themselves on the right path; and if they turn away, it is only they who will be deeply in the wrong or in schism (*shiqāq*) (2: 137).

Acceptable and Unacceptable Differences

God Almighty has ordained differences between human beings in their mental capabilities, their languages, the color of their skin, and their perceptions and thoughts. All this naturally gives rise to a multiplicity and variety of opinions and judgments. If our languages, the color of our skins, and our outer appearances are signs of God's creative power and wisdom; and if our minds, our mental capabilities, and the products of these minds are also signs of God and an indication of His consummate power; and if the populating of the universe, the beauty of being alive, and being able to live are also indications of God's power, then we can justifiably say that none of this exquisite beauty and variety among human beings would have been possible if they had been created equal in every respect. Every created being indeed has its own unique characteristics:

> If your Lord had so willed, He would have made mankind one people, but they will not cease to differ, except those on whom Your Lord and Sustainer has bestowed His mercy, and for this did He create them (11: 118-9).

The differences which occurred among our forebears in early Muslim history and which continue to be with us are part of this natural manifestation of variety. Provided that differences do not exceed their limits, and provided they remain within the standard norms of ethics and proper behavior, this is a phenomenon that could prove to be positive and extremely beneficial.

Some Benefits of Acceptable Differences

As mentioned above, if differences are confined to their proper limits and people are trained to observe the proper ethics and norms of expressing and managing differences, there are several positive advantages that could result.

If intentions are sincere, differences of opinion could bring about a greater awareness of the various possible aspects and interpretations of evidence in a given case. Such differences could generate intellectual vitality and a cross-fertilization of ideas. The process is likely to bring into the open a variety of hypotheses in tackling specific issues.

Such a process is likely to present a variety of solutions for dealing with a particular situation so that the most suitable solution can be found. This is in harmony with the facilitating nature of the religion of Islam which takes into account the reality of people's lives.

These and other benefits can be realized if differences remain within the limits and the ethical norms which must regulate them. If these limits and norms are not observed, differences could easily degenerate into disputes and schisms and become a negative and evil force producing more rifts in the Muslim Ummah, which already has more than enough of such fragmentation. In this way, differences of opinion can change from being a constructive force to being elements of destruction.

Impulsive Disagreements

Disagreement may be prompted by egoistical desires to get personal, psychological satisfaction or to achieve certain personal objectives. It may be impelled by the desire to show off one's knowledge and understanding or cleverness. To cause this type of disagreement is totally blameworthy, in that egoism or selfish desire suppresses all concern for the truth and does not promote goodness. It was such egoism that beguiled Satan and led him into disbelief. God says in the Qur'an:

> Is it not so that whenever an Apostle from God came to you with something that was not to your personal liking, you gloried in your arrogance, and some of them you called impostors while others you would slay (2: 87).

As a result of following egoistical desire, many people have swerved from dealing justly:

> Do not then follow your own desires, lest you swerve from justice (4: 135).

Following one's own desires leads to deviation and error:

> Say: I do not follow your vain desires. If I did, I would stray from the straight path and would not be among those who are rightly guided (6: 56).

Egoistical desire is the antithesis of knowledge. It seeks to stifle truth. It promotes corruption and leads to error:

> Do not follow vain desire (*hawā*) for it will mislead you from the path of God (38: 26).
>
> If the Truth were in accord with their own desires, the heavens and the earth would surely have fallen into ruin, and all that lives in them (23: 71).
>
> Many [people] lead others astray by their own [selfish] desires without having any real knowledge (6: 119).

The types of personal desire are various and stem from various sources. In general, desire springs from the ego and love of self. Such desire gives rise to many misdeeds and deviations. But a person is not easily trapped by it until every misdeed and deviation acquires a certain attractiveness in his eyes and he persists in straying. In this situation, truth appears as falsehood and falsehood appears as truth. The disputes among sects and propagators of misguided innovation in the religion of Islam can be attributed to the stranglehold of vain desire.

Through God's blessings and care a person may be made aware of the extent of the impact of vain desires on his opinions and beliefs before he is totally caught in the snares of error. Such a person may see the light of God's guidance and be made to realize that his opinions and beliefs which stem from infatuation with his own vain desires do not have any objective reality. They exist only in the mind and are illusory. They have been conjured up and made attractive by his own vain desires, however ugly and abhorrent they actually are. They are a source of affliction to the person thus ensnared.

There are various ways of detecting the effect of personal inclination on the formation of any opinion or belief. Some of these are external and some are personal. The external ways of doing so involve showing that the discordant opinion or belief is categorically opposed to a clear text of the Qur'an or the Sunnah. One would not expect a person who professes to be keen on upholding the truth to pursue an idea which contradicts the Qur'an and the Sunnah.

An opinion can also be shown to stem from personal caprice if it clashes with the considered assessment of persons with sound minds to whom people normally go for advice or arbitration. An opinion which calls for the worship of another beside God, or which rejects the application of the Sharī'ah in people's affairs, or which advocates illegal sexual intercourse, praises lying, or urges extravagance can only come from personal caprice and can only be advocated by someone who is led by evil influences.

With regard to internal ways of exposing whether an opinion stems from egotistical desire, this can be shown by reflecting not only on the source of the idea but also by questioning the justification for adopting that particular idea to the exclusion of another. It is also important to assess the prevailing circumstances which might have affected the holder of the opinion and the degree of his commitment to it should these circumstances change. One should also inquire whether there were any pressures which unconsciously led to the adoption of that course. Finally, one has to analyze the idea itself. If it appears to be shaky and unstable, oscillating erratically between strength and weakness, we should then be in no doubt that such an idea stems from vain desire and is insinuated by evil promptings. Having come to such a conclusion, a person must seek the protection of God and praise Him for making him see reality before he became bound by the shackles of egoism and personal caprice.

Some disagreements may indeed be motivated by the pursuit of knowledge and truth; selfishness and egoism may not be behind them. Such disagreements may also be spurred on by a striving for intellectual rigor and by the demands of faith. The differences between the people of faith on the one hand and disbelievers, polytheists, and hypocrites on the other is a necessary difference which no believing Muslim can shake off or attempt to reconcile. This is a difference required by faith and the preservation of truth. The same applies to the Muslim attitude towards atheism, Judaism, Christianity, paganism, and communism. However, the disagreement with these ideologies should not hinder the call to remove the underlying causes of such disagreement. This is in order that the way may be left open for people to embrace Islam and abandon the mainsprings of disbelief, worshipping others beside God, hypocrisy, schism and immorality, atheism and innovation, and the promotion of beliefs which are destructive of truth and goodness.

Differences among Muslims are also fostered by apportioning praise or blame over minor issues, often with little regard for genuine sincerity. Rulings on these issues allow for alternative opinions or practices. How this came about will be examined in a later chapter. Some examples of such disagreements concern the differences among the *'ulamā'* with regard to the nullification of ablution (*wuḍū'*) by blood from a wound or by induced vomiting; about reciting the Qur'an aloud in ṣalāh after the imam; saying *Bismillāhi al Raḥmānī al Raḥīm* at the beginning of *al Fātiḥah*, the opening chapter of the Qur'an; and saying *āmīn* aloud after the recitation of *al Fātiḥah*. There are many other such examples.

Disagreement over such subsidiary issues are often quite sensitive and may lead a person to confuse piety with his own personal inclination, knowledge with conjecture, the preferable with what he himself has chosen, and the acceptable with the unacceptable. Such disagreements are inevitable unless we have recourse to agreed-upon criteria for resolving them, disciplines to regulate the methods of deduction, and ethical norms which would govern the conduct of handling differences. Otherwise, there would be a drift to wrangling, schism, and ultimate failure. In such a case, both parties in any dispute would slip from a position of piety and God-consciousness to the abyss of egoistical desires. The floodgates of chaos and anarchy would be opened and Satan would thrive.

Discord is Evil

It is important to emphasize that from early post-Qur'anic history, leading Muslim scholars have warned against disagreement in all its forms and emphasized that it is essential to avoid it. The companion of the Prophet, Ibn Mas'ūd—may God be pleased with him—said: "Discord (*khilāf*) is evil."[3] Al Subkī, may God be merciful to him, said: "Kindness and compassion (*raḥmah*) require that you should eschew disagreement."

3. See Ibn Qutaybah, *Ta'wīl Mukhtalif al Hadīth*, p. 22; *Al 'Awāṣim min al Qawāṣim*, p. 78; *al Maḥṣūl*, 2/Qafl/480.

There are many verses of the Qur'an and many sayings of the Prophet, peace be upon him, in this regard. The Qur'an speaks of people who contended with one another after all evidence of truth had come to them, but as it was, "they did take to divergent views, and some of them attained to faith, while some of them came to deny the truth" (2: 253). And the Prophet, peace and blessings of God be on him, has said: "The Israelites perished only because of their excessive questioning and their disputes over their prophets."[4]

Al Subkī lists three types of differences in dealing with minor issues over which people indulge in mutual blame and praise. The first, which he regarded as innovation and straying from the straight path, concerns the very sources of Islam. The second concerns opinions freely expressed and (internecine) wars; this type of disagreement is also forbidden because it is injurious to the public interest. The third concerns subsidiary matters with respect to what is lawful and what is prohibited.[5] He concluded that agreement on these is better than disagreement. He also drew attention to Ibn Ḥazm's deprecation of disagreement on such issues in which he did not perceive any blessing but regarded the whole process as a scourge.

It is indicative of the harmful and dangerous consequences of disagreement that the Prophet Hārūn, on whom be peace, considered disagreement and discord (*ikhtilāf*) at a given moment as more dangerous and more harmful than the outright condemnation of idol worship. When someone (called the Sāmirī in the Qur'an) made a golden calf for the Israelites and said to them: "This is your god and the god of Mūsā" (20: 88), Hārūn pointed out to them the grave consequences of what they were being led into but waited for his brother Mūsā—peace be on him—to return. When Mūsā came and saw the people worshipping the golden calf, he rebuked his brother most severely. His brother's only reply was to say:

> Son of my mother! Seize me not by my beard nor by the hair of my head! Truly I was afraid that you would say, 'You have

4. The complete ḥadīth is reported by Abū Hurayrah: "Do not bother with what I have omitted. Those before you perished only because of their excessive questioning and their disputes over their prophets. When I enjoin anything on you, carry it out to the best of your ability and if I forbid you from anything, let it alone." Transmitted by Aḥmad in his *Musnad*, and by Muslim, al Nasā'ī and Ibn Mājah.

5. See *al Ibhāj*, 3/13.

caused a division among the Children of Israel, and you did not respect my word' (20: 94).

The Prophet Hārūn thus made the fear of division and disagreement among his people his justification for not severely reprimanding the Israelites, resisting them, and distancing himself from them. He felt that that was a time when outright condemnation would be counter-productive, not beneficial, and would lead to disagreement and disunity.

Chapter Three

The Historical Context (1)

In the Prophet's Lifetime

Such disagreement as we have mentioned in the previous chapter could not have taken place during the time of the Prophet, may God bless him and grant him peace. He was universally acknowledged by all his Companions as the one to whom any controversial matter had to be referred. He was their source of refuge and solace and their guide whenever they were perplexed. He would clarify issues for them and show the way to truth and offer right guidance.

Those who lived far away from Madinah and could not refer matters directly to the Prophet—matters such as the correct interpretation of the Qur'an and the Sunnah in the light of the knowledge they had—would exercise their own judgment and sometimes came to differing conclusions. When they returned to Madinah, however, they would meet the Prophet and review with him their different interpretations of the texts available to them. The Prophet would either approve of a particular judgment which then became part of his Sunnah, or he would point out the correct alternative which they would adopt wholeheartedly. Any disagreement or friction automatically disappeared.

One example of such an incident has been recorded by both al Bukhārī and Muslim. During the Battle of the Confederates, the Prophet is reported to have said to his Companions: "Do not perform the mid-afternoon (*'aṣr*) *ṣalāh* until you get to the [place of] Banū Qurayẓah." While still on their way, the time of the *ṣalāh* came. Some of the companions said, "We will not perform the *ṣalāh* until we get to the [place of] Banū Qurayẓah" while some others said, "We shall pray. That [saying of the Prophet] will not prevent us [from praying now]." The matter was later brought before the Prophet and he did not disapprove of either group.[1]

It is clear from this incident that the Companions of the Prophet had split into two groups over the interpretation of the Prophet's instructions – one group adopting the literal or explicit meaning of the injunction (*'ibārat al naṣṣ*) while the other group derived a meaning from the injunction which they considered suitable for that situation. The fact that the Prophet approved of both groups showed that each position was legally just as valid as the other.

Thus, a Muslim who is faced with a particular injunction or text (*naṣṣ*) can either adopt the literal or manifest (*ẓāhir*) meaning of the text or he may derive interpretations which are appropriate to the text by using his reason. This latter process of inference or deriving an interpretation in order to ascertain the real intention behind an injunction is called *istinbāṭ*. There is no blame attached to the one who strives to use it provided he is qualified and competent to do so. The second group of Companions understood from the Prophet's injunction that he wanted to get to their destination as quickly as possible. They therefore considered that their performing of the prayer before reaching the Banū Qurayẓah did not contradict the order of the Prophet, so long as this did not delay their arrival unduly.

It is disconcerting to note that Ibn al Qayyim reported on differing views of various scholars on this issue in an attempt to show which group acted better. One set of scholars expressed the view that the group which acted better was the one that prayed on the way, thus attaining the reward of performing the *ṣalāh* on time while carrying out the Prophet's injunction. Another set of scholars argued that those who delayed the prayer in order to perform it at the place of Banū Qurayẓah – according to the exact letter of the law or injunction – deserved more merit.[2] However, I believe that as long as the Prophet himself did not disapprove of either group, it is incumbent on jurists to regard both positions as being a valid part of the Sunnah of the Prophet and to refrain from getting embroiled in an issue which the Prophet himself had resolved by leaving no room for any further preference.

---

1. See *Fatḥ al Bārī* commentary on *Ṣaḥīḥ al Bukhārī*, 7/313; *Ṣaḥīḥ Muslim*, the *Book of al Ṣalāh*.

2. Ibn al Qayyim, *I'lām al Muwaqqi'īn*.

Another incident in this same vein has been recorded by Abū Dāwūd and al Ḥākim. It is reported that 'Amr ibn al 'Āṣ, may God be pleased with him, said:

> One cold night during the Dhāt al Salāsil[3] campaign, I had a wet dream. I feared that if I performed *ghusl* [necessary bath after ritual impurity] I would die [from the cold]. So I performed *tayammum* [dry ablution] instead, then performed the dawn *ṣalāh* with my companions. This was mentioned to the Prophet who asked: 'Amr! You performed the prayer with your companions while you were in a state of impurity [*junub*]?' Whereupon I recalled to him the verse of the Qur'ān: 'And kill not yourselves. Indeed God has been most Merciful to you.' The Prophet laughed and said nothing.[4]

The Interpretive Process

We shall not concern ourselves here with detailing the various issues on which the Companions differed during and after the lifetime of the Prophet. Nor shall we detail on each issue who adopted the literal or obvious meaning of a text on the one hand and who reflected on and scrutinized its various aspects and derived various interpretations from it on the other. Such an undertaking would require volumes. Moreover, it must be borne in mind that the Companions themselves appreciated in all these circumstances that the religion of Islam was easy and that the law was wide enough to accommodate both approaches and methods.

It was the proficient scholars (*mujtahidūn*; singular: *mujtahid*) who were capable of analytical thought and of making independent judgments, and the skilled jurists (*fuqahā'*; singular: *faqīh*) who painstakingly strove to investigate the full ramifications of the Sharī'ah and set out its purposes. Sometimes they would adopt the literal or manifest meaning of an expression and sometimes they would adopt an interpretation that went beyond this. This interpretive process is called *ta'wīl*. It may be useful to shed some light on the various types of *ta'wīl* and the conditions for it.

---

3. A place on the Syrian borders.

4. Abū Dāwūd, *Sunan*, ḥadīth 334; *Fatḥ al Bārī* commentary of Ṣaḥīḥ al Bukhārī, 1/385; *Nayl al Awṭār*, 1/324.

Briefly, this interpretive process may be divided into three types: close or plausible interpretation (*ta'wīl qarīb*); remote interpretation (*ta'wīl ba'īd*); and far-fetched interpretation (*ta'wīl mustab'ad*).

Plausible Interpretation

A close or plausible interpretation is one which can easily be sustained from the import of a text. For example, giving to charity funds appropriated from an orphan's trust or wasting such funds can both be construed as tantamount to "eating up the property of orphans" and therefore regarded as acts prohibited by the Qur'an: "Those who eat up the property of orphans only eat fire in their bellies" (4: 10).

Remote Interpretation

A remote interpretation is one which requires a far greater degree of pondering and probing into the substance of a text. An example of this is the deduction (*istinbāṭ*) of Ibn 'Abbās from the following Qur'anic verses that the minimum period of human pregnancy is six months:

> The [mother's] bearing of the [child] and his weaning is [a period of] thirty months (46: 15).
>
> Mothers may nurse their children for two whole years if they wish to complete the period of nursing (2: 233).

Another example of such interpretation is the inference of Imām al Shāfi'ī from the following Qur'anic verse that consensus (*ijmā'*) is admissible as a proof of the validity of a ruling:

> But as for him who, after guidance has been vouchsafed to him, cuts himself off from the Apostle and follows a path other than that of the believers, him shall We leave unto that which he himself has chosen, and We shall cause him to endure hell; and how evil a journey's end (4: 115).

In the same manner, jurists have inferred that analogical reasoning or deduction (*qiyās*) is admissible as a proof of the validity of a ruling from the verse: "Learn a lesson, then, O you who are endowed with insight" (59: 2).

Such inferences and deductions, even though they may seem easy, are difficult to arrive at unless a person is engaged in thought and has a penetrating insight. It involves, moreover, a great deal of critical research. It is not an easy task for most people.

Far-Fetched Interpretation

Such an interpretation cannot be construed from the text itself and the interpreter does not possess any shred of evidence to support his interpretation. An example of such an interpretation concerns the verse:

> And he has placed on earth . . . rivers and paths that you might find your way, and means of orientation; and by the stars that men find their way (16: 15-16).

Some commentators have suggested that the word *'alāmāt* ('means of orientation') refers to the *a'immah* and the word *al najm* or 'the stars' refers to the Prophet Muhammad, peace be on him. Similarly, with regard to the verse: "But neither signs (*āyāt*) nor warners (*nudhur*) profit a people who do not believe" (10: 101), some commentators have suggested that the word *āyāt* refers to the *a'immah* or scholarly leaders, and the word *nudhur* to the prophets.

Also with regard to the verses: "About what do they ask one another? About the great news" (78: 1-2), some commentators have suggested that "the great news" refers to 'Alī, may God be pleased with him. [5]

Rules of Interpretation

It is clear from what we have said that interpretation requires an ability to ponder and reflect on the real import and purpose of a text. Otherwise it is safer to adopt the more obvious and manifest meanings. Interpretation is only admissible in matters on which there is no clear guidance in the Qur'an and the Sunnah and which require the use of rigorous reasoning (ijtihād). In matters pertaining to belief there is no room for ijtihād, and it is necessary to adopt the manifest meanings and what is properly and strictly sanctioned by the purport of the text. This

5. See *Uṣūl al Kāfī*, 1/216.

is always the safest method and one which the early Muslims followed.

However, there are texts which require interpretation. In this case, the text at issue must be fully analyzed and understood. This requires a thorough knowledge of all the pertinent linguistic implications. This must be underpinned by a constant awareness of the purposes of the Sharī'ah and the principles which regulate it. In light of all this, the act of making a judgment, whether through considering the explicit meaning of a text or analyzing it with respect to the pertinent principles and proofs, is one of the most important types of juristic reasoning (*al ijtihād al fiqhī*) and legal intellectual effort required by the divine injunction: "Learn a lesson, then, O you who are endowed with insight" (59: 2).

In dealing with rules and conditions of Qur'anic exegesis or commentary (*tafsīr*), the knowledgeable Companion of the Prophet, Ibn 'Abbas, mentioned four aspects:

- the aspect pertaining to the knowledge and understanding of Arabic usage;
- the aspect which no one is excused through ignorance;
- the aspect known by the *'ulamā'*;
- the aspect known only by God.

From what has been said above, there is a firm connection between *ta'wīl* and *tafsīr*. Both terms occur interchangeably in many instances in the Qur'an, for example:

> But no one knows its interpretation (*ta'wīl*) except God. And those who are firmly rooted in knowledge say: 'We believe in it' (3: 7).

Most commentators of the Qur'an are of the view that *ta'wīl* in the above verse refers to interpretation (*tafsīr*) and explanation (*bayān*). Among these commentators is al Ṭabarī, who transmitted this view on the authority of Ibn 'Abbās and other early Muslims. That *ta'wīl* is synonymous with *tafsīr* is also borne out by the Prophet's prayer for Ibn 'Abbās: "O Allah, give him a firm understanding (fiqh) of the religion and teach him interpretation (*ta'wīl*)." Some scholars like al Raghīb al Isfahānī in his book *Mufradāt* (Glossary) considered *tafsīr* to be more general than *ta'wīl*, and also alluded to the fact that the word *tafsīr* is more frequently used for the explanation and elucidation of terms while *ta'wīl* is more often used to explain meanings and sentences. He also pointed out that *ta'wīl* is more often than not used for deriving (*istinbāṭ*) meanings from texts of the Qur'an and Sunnah while *tafsīr* draws upon these and other sources as well to derive meanings.

This strong connection between the two terms – as used in the Qur'an and Sunnah especially – allows us to apply the rules developed for *tafsīr* to those which also concern *ta'wīl*.

There is no doubt that the Qur'an contains matters of which knowledge is reserved for God alone – matters pertaining to knowledge of the true meaning of God's names and attributes, to the details of all that is beyond the reach of human perception included in the term *al ghayb*. There are other matters which God has revealed to Prophet Muḥammad and only he knew about them. No one has the right or the ability to delve into the interpretation and explanation of these matters; commenting on them must remain within the limits of what is stated in the Qur'an and Sunnah.

There is yet a third category of subjects which deal with sciences which God has revealed to the Prophet in the Qur'an and commissioned him to teach and explain. This category consists of two types. The first relates to matters which can only be delved into through the sense of hearing – like the circumstances surrounding the revelation of a particular portion of the Qur'an (*asbāb al nuzūl*) and matters pertaining to the abrogation of verses (*al nāsikh wa al mansūkh*) and so on. The second relates to matters which can be grasped through insight, reason, and advancing proofs. Scholars are divided into two groups in their approach to this. One group did not allow interpretation of the verses of the Qur'an which made reference to the names and attributes of God. The early Muslims also prohibited such interpretation. This is the correct stand. A second group agreed that interpretation was permissible and that legal rules could be derived from the texts supported by detailed evidence. This discipline is known as jurisprudence or fiqh (which literally means 'understanding').

The *'ulamā'* have accordingly established conditions for the exercise of interpretation (*ta'wīl*) and explanation (*tafsīr*):

1. Interpretation should not disregard the explicit (*ẓāhir*) connotation of a word as understood in accordance with the accepted rules of the language and the speech norms of the Arabs.
2. Interpretation should not contradict a Qur'anic text.
3. Interpretation must not be at variance with a juristic prin-

ciple established by a consensus of the *'ulamā'* and the *a'immah*.

4. The necessity to strictly observe the purpose behind the text or injunction in the circumstances it was revealed or mentioned.

As for the false and untenable kinds of interpretation (*ta'wīl*), these may be conveniently listed as follows:

1. Interpretations and explanations made by persons not qualified for the task, who do not have sufficient knowledge of Arabic language and grammar nor of the other requisites of interpretation.
2. Interpretation of intricate or allegorical texts (*mutashābihāt*) whose meaning is totally unclear without the backing of authentic evidence.
3. Interpretations that seek to establish corrupt ideologies which go against the explicit teachings of the Qur'an and the Sunnah or the consensus (*ijmā'*) of the Muslims.
4. Interpretation, without any evidence, which definitely attributes a purpose to the Lawgiver.
5. Interpretation based on pure conjecture such as the interpretations of the esoteric sects like the Bāṭinīyah and others.

All these categories of interpretation are rejected and fall under the previously mentioned category of far-fetched interpretations.

The Companions and Ijtihad

In view of the critical importance of ijtihād and the processes involved in it, only the qualified and capable Companions of the Prophet practiced it. When others engaged in ijtihād and erred, the Prophet, peace be on him, rejected what they had done and did not encourage such risks. The following account narrated by Jābir, a Companion of the Prophet, demonstrates this:

> We went out on a journey and one of our men was hit on the head by a stone. He then had a wet dream and so asked

> his companions: 'Can you find a ruling which would give me a dispensation to make dry ablution (*tayammum*) [instead of having to take a bath]?' They replied: 'We do not find any dispensation for you while you can obtain water.' So he had the bath but subsequently died. When we got back to the Messenger of God and told him what had happened, he, may the peace and blessings of God be on him, said: 'They killed him. May God kill them. Why did they not ask if they did not know? The cure for the incapable one is merely to ask. It would have been sufficient for the deceased simply to make *tayammum*, or he could have bandaged his wound and passed his wet hand lightly over the bandaged area and then washed the rest of his body.' [6]

It is clear from this ḥadīth that the Prophet did not absolve his Companions who made a legal ruling without having the knowledge and the competence to do so. Instead, he reprimanded them sharply and blamed them for making a legal decision without knowledge. He considered them as murderers of their brother in faith. Furthermore, he made it plain that it was incumbent on those like them who were incapable – that is who were ignorant and confused in such matters – to ask and not to rush to give a verdict (*fatwā*). The Prophet's insistence on the necessity of asking in such circumstances is supported by the divine injunction: "Ask the knowledgeable if you do not know" (16: 43).

Usāmah ibn Zayd related the following incident:

> The Messenger of God, may God bless him and grant him peace, sent us on a military expedition and we fell under fire from [the tribe of] Juhaynah. I confronted a man and he declared, 'There is no god but Allah (*lā ilāha illā Allāh*)' but I stabbed him. This troubled me immensely and I mentioned it to the Prophet, may God bless him and grant him peace. The Messenger of God, may God bless him and grant him peace, asked: 'Did he say *lā ilāha illā Allāh* and you killed him?' I said: 'O Messenger of Allah, he only said it out of fear of the weapon.' The Prophet said: 'Did you open his heart

6. Abū Dāwūd, *Sunan*, ḥadīth 336; also transmitted by Ibn Mājah, ḥadīth 572; see *Nayl al Awṭār*, 1/323.

> in order to know that that is why he uttered it [the profession of faith: the *shahādah*] or not? Who will be on your side on the Day of Judgment when this *lā ilāha illā Allāh* is pronounced?' He continued repeating this so that I wished I had not embraced Islam before that day."[7]

In the first ḥadīth, the Prophet rejected the judgment of the Companions in that it was based on the general evidence which made it obligatory for a Muslim to use water for ablution when it is available while ignoring the specific condition of the person. In this respect, they did not pay attention to the Qur'anic verse:

> If you are sick or are on a journey, or have just satisfied a demand of nature, or have had contact with a woman and can find no water, then take resort to clean sand or earth. God does not want to impose any hardship on you, but wants to make you pure (5: 6).

Moreover, they were not knowledgeable people and they did not ask. In the incident concerning Usāmah, it seems that he did what he did in the light of his interpretation of the Qur'anic verse: "But their professing the faith when they (actually) saw our punishment was not going to benefit them" (40: 85). He therefore considered that this verse negated any benefit for the person concerned in this world and in the hereafter and that it was not specifically concerned with the hereafter, which is the obvious meaning of the verse. Perhaps it was this which made the Prophet censure him so strongly.

These are just some examples of the verdicts (*fatāwā*; singular: *fatwā*) reached by the companions, may God be pleased with them, which the Prophet did not validate.[8]

People would come to the Prophet to seek his ruling on actual incidents and he would answer their questions. Various issues and problems were presented to him to settle and he would do so.[9] He would see a good deed and commend it and praise its door. He would see a

---

7. Transmitted by al Imām Aḥmad, al Bukhārī, Muslim, al Nasā'ī, al Ṭabarānī. Also transmitted by al Bukhārī, 7/398, with some variation.

8. Ibn Ḥazm has recorded a number of verdicts (*fatāwā*) of the Companions which the Prophet did not validate. See his *al Iḥkam*, 6/84-5 and 2/126-7.

9. See *Ḥujjat Allāh al Bālighah*, 1/298.

reprehensible act and disapprove of it. Those of his Companions who were present would learn directly from the Prophet and in turn would pass on what they had learnt to others. In the process they might differ among themselves, but they would continue to discuss any controversial issues in an objective manner and in such a way that did not lead to discord and schism or nasty accusations. This was because they would always go back to the Book of God and His Messenger, may God bless him and grant him peace. They would put a decisive end to any disagreement such that no trace of ill-feeling was left to weaken the bond of brotherhood among them.

Disagreement and the Prophet's Warning

The Prophet warned his Companions about the dangers of disagreement. He realized that the survival of the Ummah depended on the harmony and mutual affection of the believers, whose hearts had come together on the basis of love for God. He also realized that the ruin of the Ummah lay in the hearts of believers torn by mutual strife. So the Prophet, peace and blessings of God be on him, repeatedly warned that discord should cease to raise its head and therefore said: "Do not engage in disagreement thereby causing discord among your hearts."[10]

The Companions of the Prophet themselves saw that discord produced nothing good. Ibn Mas'ūd, may God be pleased with him, once said: "Disagreement is evil." Furthermore, the Prophet would always nip any disagreement in the bud, as the following incident narrated by 'Abd Allāh ibn 'Umar shows. He said:

> One day I called upon the Messenger of God, may God bless him and grant him peace, during the midday rest. [While I was there], the Prophet heard two men arguing loudly in disagreement over [the meaning of a Qur'anic verse]. The Messenger of God, may God bless him and grant him peace, went out with anger showing on his face and said: 'People before you perished only because of their disagreement about the Scripture.'[11]

Al Nazzāl ibn Sabrah related:

---

10. Al Bukhārī in *al Jāmi' al Ṣaghīr*, 2/494.
11. Ibn Ḥazm, *al Iḥkām*, 5/66.

> I heard 'Abd Allāh ibn Mas'ūd saying, 'I heard a man reciting a verse from the Qur'an which I had heard from God's Messenger, but differently. I took him by the hand and brought him to the Messenger of God who said: "Both of you have done good." Shu'bah added, "I think he [also] said: 'Do not engage in disagreement, for those before you engaged in disagreement and perished."[12]

Here the Prophet instructed his Companions and those who come after them about the dire consequences of disagreement and warned them against it. The Prophet also taught his Companions about the crucial manner in which they had to observe the ethics of disagreement, especially in reciting the Qur'an. In an authentic ḥadīth, he has said: "Read [and study] the Qur'an so long as your hearts are united on it, but when you have differences over it, stop [your recitation]."[13]

In the event of disagreement arising over different modes of reciting the Qur'an or over the intended meaning of any of its verses, the Prophet, peace be on him, charged his Companions to stand away from the glorious Qur'an until they were completely calm and all the stimuli of acrimonious argument which lead to discord and schism had been quelled. On the other hand, when their hearts were united, a sincere desire to understand prevailed and they could then continue with their reading, reflection, and pondering on the verses of the Qur'an. We also see that the Qur'an itself sometimes issued a caution regarding the ethics of disagreement when it occurred among the Companions. In this context, 'Abd Allāh ibn al Zubayr is reported to have said:

> The two chosen Companions of the Prophet, Abū Bakr and 'Umar, may God be pleased with them, almost ruined themselves. They both raised their voices in the presence of the Prophet, peace be on him, when a delegation of the Banū Tamīm came to him. One of the two men recommended al Aqra' ibn Ḥābīs [to be appointed the chief of the delegation] while the other pointed to al-Qa'qā' ibn Ma'bad ibn Zarārah.

---

12. See Ibn Ḥazm, *Al Iḥkām*. Also *Ṣaḥīḥ al Bukhārī* in the chapter on "The Repugnance of Disagreement" (Bāb Karāhīyat al Ikhtilāf), 13/289.

13. Transmitted by al Bukhārī and Muslim, Aḥmad in his *Musnad*, and by al Nasā'ī.

Abū Bakr thereupon said to 'Umar: 'You only wanted to oppose me.' 'Umar replied: 'I did not want to oppose you.' Their voices grew louder and louder over the issue. And the divine words were revealed: 'O you who have attained to faith, do not raise your voices above the voice of the Prophet' (49: 2-3). Ibn al Zubayr added: 'After the revelation of this verse, 'Umar would scarcely make himself heard by the Prophet; so much so that the Prophet would have to ask him to repeat his words.'[14]

Salient Features

In the light of the above, we can list some of the salient features of the ethics of disagreement during the time of the Prophet:

1. The Companions, may God be pleased with them, tried as far as possible not to disagree. They did not make much about marginal issues[15] but treated the matters that posed controversy in the light of the Prophet's guidance. This manner of dealing with actual situations normally does not leave much room for argumentation, let alone dispute and discord.
2. If differences occurred despite attempts to avoid them, the Companions would quickly refer the disputed issue to the Qur'an and to the Prophet, and any controversy would be quickly dispelled.
3. The Companions reacted with a ready obedience and commitment to the judgment of the Qur'an and the Prophet and their complete and total submission to it.
4. The Prophet used to point out to his Companions what was right and what was wrong with regards to controversial questions open to interpretation. On their part, the Companions had mutual trust in the genuineness of each other's judgments. This approach guaranteed the preservation of mutual respect among fellow Muslims who differed, and also kept fanaticism and bigotry at bay.

14. Transmitted by al Bukhārī—see *Fatḥ al Bārī*, 8/66, 454 and 13/235.
15. Ibid., 13/219-28.

5. Commitment to God-consciousness and avoidance of personal whims made the pursuit of truth alone the goal of those who differed over an issue. It did not matter to anyone in a discussion whether the truth was voiced by him or by another person.
6. They adhered steadfastly to the Islamic norms of behavior during argumentation. They discussed matters politely and amicably, avoiding the use of vile and insulting language. Each was prepared to listen attentively to the other.
7. They eschewed hypocrisy and flattery as far as possible and exerted every effort to investigate an issue objectively. This practice, characterized by the seriousness of the argument and respect for the other person, would force the disputant into either accepting the other point of view or advancing a better opinion.

Chapter Four

The Historical Context (2)

The First Generation

Some writers on Islam and Muslim history try to portray the generation of the Companions in a way that causes people to believe it was not only unique but inimitable—that it is impossible to have such a generation again. This is an affront to Islam no less serious than the misguided claim that after the Companions it is impossible to reconstruct Islamic life according to the teachings of the Qur'an and the Sunnah and therefore futile to strive towards this goal. In this way, misguided persons attempt to stifle the aspirations of those who still continue to pursue the goal of a life in the shade of the protective Sharī'ah.

The Companions were a community (Ummah) molded by the Book of God and the Sunnah of His Messenger, both of which are available to us and are capable of creating a God-fearing Ummah in any time and in any place when they are adopted as a program and a method, and when people relate to them in the same manner as did the Companions. This will remain true until the Day of Judgment. To allege that it is impossible to reconstruct a generation like that of the Companions is to attribute some measure of deficiency to the Qur'an and the Sunnah of the Prophet. Such a claim also seeks to suggest that the impact of the Qur'an and the Sunnah on the lives of people in that generation was conditioned on specific circumstances existing at that time. They argue that these circumstances are irrelevant to the present age which has introduced new systems appropriate to the new circumstances. This is an argument that ultimately leads to manifest unbelief and rejection (*kufr*) of Islam.

The Companions of the Prophet indeed differed on many issues. If these differences occurred during the lifetime of the Prophet, why should they not have differed after him? In fact they did differ. But there were reasons for their differences, and there were ethics in dealing with those differences which concerned issues of grave importance.

After the Death of the Prophet

The first disagreement among the Companions after the death of the Prophet concerned the reality of his death itself. 'Umar ibn al Khaṭṭāb, may God be pleased with him, insisted that the Messenger of God did not die, considered any such talk a false rumor spread by the hypocrites, and threatened to punish them for it. This went on until Abū Bakr appeared on the scene and recited the verse of the Qur'an:

> Muḥammad is no more than a Messenger. Many were the Messengers who passed away before him. If he died or were slain, will you then turn back on your heels? Whoever turns back on his heels, not the least harm will he do to God; but God [on the other hand] will swiftly reward those who [serve him] with gratitude (3: 144).

And another verse of the Qur'an:

> Truly you will die [one day], and truly they [too] will die [one day] (39: 30).

When 'Umar heard these verses his sword fell from his hand and he himself fell to the ground. He realized that the Prophet, may God bless him and grant him peace, had passed away and that the divine revelation had come to an end. About the verses which Abū Bakr had recited, he said: "By God, it seems to me as if I had never read these verses before."[1]

Ibn 'Abbās reported that 'Umar ibn al Khaṭṭāb during his caliphate told him:

> "O Ibn 'Abbās, do you know what made me say what I said when the Messenger of Allah, peace be on him, passed away?" I replied: "I do not know, O Amīr al Mu'minīn. You know better." 'Umar then said: "By God, the only thing which made me say that was this verse of the Qur'an I used to read: 'Thus have We made of you an Ummah justly balanced, that you might be witnesses over people, and the Prophet is a witness

1. See Ibn Ḥazm, *al Iḥkām*, 2/125; Ibn Kathīr, *Tafsīr*, 4/52 al Ṭabarī, *Tafsīr*, 24/302; Ibn Hishām, *Sīrah*, 2/655.

over you' (2: 143). By God, I used to think that the Prophet, peace be on him, would remain among his Ummah so that he could be a witness over it till the last of its deeds. That is what made me say what I said."[2]

It seems that 'Umar had made an independent interpretation of the verse and concluded that "witnessing" applied to the whole span of life in this world. This would have required the Prophet to remain alive till the end of the Ummah's days.

Differences over the Prophet's Burial

The second issue on which the Companions differed concerned the place where the Prophet should be buried. One person said: "We should bury him in his mosque." Another said: "We should bury him next to his Companions." Abū Bakr then said: "I heard the Messenger of God, may God bless him and grant him peace, say: 'Whenever a prophet died he was buried where he died.'" Thereupon, the bed on which the Prophet died was raised and his grave was dug beneath it.[3]

These were two critical issues which were swiftly resolved simply by resorting to the Qur'an and the Sunnah.

Who Should Succeed the Prophet?

Another controversy arose about who was to succeed the Prophet. Should the successor be from among the Muhajirūn (emigrants from Makkah) or from the Anṣār (helpers from Madinah)? Should the office be entrusted to one person or more? Should the successor be vested with the same prerogatives exercised by the Prophet in his capacity as judge and leader (imām) of the Muslims, or should these prerogatives be less or different?

Ibn Isḥāq reports in this respect:

---

2. Ibn Hishām, *Sīrah*, 2/661, 666. It is related that 'Umar ibn al Khaṭṭāb said something similar when he gave his oath of allegiance (*bay'ah*) to Abū Bakr in the Prophet's mosque.

3. Ibid. Also al Tirmidhī, *Sunan*, ḥadīth 1018.

When the Prophet passed away, a group of Anṣār assembled at the meeting place of Banū Sā'idah and sided with Sa'd ibn 'Ubādah. 'Alī ibn Abū Ṭālib, al Zubayr ibn al 'Awwām, and Ṭalḥah ibn 'Ubayd Allāh gathered together in Fāṭimah's house. The rest of the Muhājirūn sided with Abū Bakr and so did Usayd ibn Ḥuḍayr among the Banū 'Abd al Ashhal.[4]

A great civil strife was about to occur. If it had occurred, it would not have been a great surprise. The demise of the Prophet with his tremendous personality and his status as a Prophet and leader created a vacuum which it was not possible to fill easily. This was especially so because there were some Companions like 'Umar ibn al-Khaṭṭāb who had held the Prophet in such high esteem that he could not believe his death. Every individual in the community loved the Prophet more than he loved himself—so much so that while the Prophet was performing ablution, they would stretch out their hands to catch some droplets before the water of his ablution fell to the ground. Indeed no community has ever loved its Prophet and its leader as much as the Companions loved the Messenger of God. In spite of the Prophet's extreme humility, none of his Companions could look him straight in the eyes. Such was both their love for him and their awe of him. The shock of the Prophet's death was capable of making them lose their wits. Indeed this is what happened and there is nothing strange about it. It was through the Prophet's loving care that they manage to secure dignity and prosperity in this world and felicity in the hereafter. In spite of this they were able to overcome their agonizing grief and the pain of separation as they recited the words of God Almighty: "Muḥammad is no more than a messenger. Many were the messengers that passed away before him. If he died or were slain, will you then turn back on your heels? Whoever turns back on his heels, not the least harm will he do to God; but God [on the other hand] will swiftly reward those who [serve him] with gratitude" (3: 144).

---

4. Ibn Hishām, *Sīrah*, 2/656-61.

Thus consoled, they directed their efforts towards resolving the problem at hand, preserving the eternal message and preventing the causes of dissension (*fitnah*).

Admittedly, there were many indications during the Prophet's lifetime that the leadership would go to Abū Bakr and then to 'Umar ibn al Khaṭṭāb. No other Muslim would aspire to or claim equal footing with these two men. Abū Bakr was the Prophet's deputy, his closest friend, his companion during the migration (*hijrah*) from Makkah to Madinah, and the father of his favorite wife, 'Ā'ishah. Abū Bakr was the one who did not forsake the Prophet in any major matter. And who was 'Umar? He was that person whose acceptance of Islam brought dignity to the Muslims, whose emigration was a source of awe and humiliation to the disbelieving Quraysh, and whose opinion received divine validation in the Qur'an. How often are such sentences as the following mentioned in the books of hadith: "The Prophet, peace be on him, came and with him were Abū Bakr and 'Umar . . ." "The Messenger of God went and with him were Abū Bakr and 'Umar . . ." or "The Messenger of God, may God bless him and grant him peace, went on an expedition and with him were Abū Bakr and 'Umar." All of this might have lessened the impact of the devastating loss felt by the Muslims. In such circumstances feelings of loss could, however, outweigh the strengths and virtues which distinguished the Companions and bring about an uncontrollable state of chaos and civil strife. Happily, the men who were brought up in and nourished by the teachings of the Prophet's message were strongly governed by its rules of conduct in all situations—whether in agreement or in disagreement, and in all aspects of life. These ethics and rules of behavior were a guarantee against all types of anticipated dangers; they guaranteed the intact preservation of the Islamic message and the protection of the unity of the Ummah. These ethics and rules ensured that the affairs of the Ummah were run in the same way as they were run during the lifetime of the Prophet.

In this respect it is narrated that someone came to Abū Bakr and 'Umar and said: "A certain group of the Anṣār are now gathering in the meeting place of Banū Sā'idah. They have sided up with Sa'd ibn 'Ubādah. If you are concerned about the affairs of the Ummah, hasten to these people before the matter gets out of control." This piece of news reached Abū Bakr and 'Umar before the body of the Prophet, peace be on him, was ready for burial. On hearing it, 'Umar said to Abū Bakr: "Let us go to these our brothers from among the Anṣār to see what they are about." 'Umar related what happened next. He said:

> The Anṣār diverged from us and held a meeting with their respected members in the meeting place of Banū Sā'idah. So we set out to join them. On the way there we met two pious men from the Anṣār who mentioned to us what their people had in mind. They asked: 'Where are you heading for, O company of Muhājirīn?' We said: 'We are going to these our brothers from the Ansar.' They said: 'You should not approach them, O company of the Muhājirūn. Decide the matter yourselves.' I said: 'By God, we shall certainly go to them.' So we set off till we came to them in the meeting place of Banū Sā'idah and there behind us was a man wrapped up. I asked: 'Who is this man?' They replied: 'Sa'd ibn 'Ubādah.' I asked: 'What's wrong with him?' They replied: 'He is ill.'
>
> We sat down listening to their spokesman who mentioned the merits and virtues of the Anṣār and suggested that they were more deserving of succeeding the Prophet than anybody else.

It is necessary to stop here and reflect on this. The Anṣār were the indigenous people of Madinah. They were also in an absolute majority. They were the ones who gave refuge and support to the Prophet and the Muhājirūn. They "who had their abode in this realm and in faith" (59: 9) opened up their hearts to Islam before they opened up their homes to the Muhājirūn. There was not a single muhājir who did not owe a tremendous debt to his Anṣāri brother in faith. If there were a categorical text in the Qur'an or the Sunnah on the issue of succession, any controversy in this respect would have been resolved by referring it to the Qur'an and the Sunnah. But as there was no text, the only way to get out of this crisis was to exercise the qualities of wisdom (*ḥikmah*) and experience, to apply the ethics of disagreement and quiet reasoned discourse. Such were the thoughts that surged through 'Umar's mind as he listened to the spokesman of the Anṣār.

'Umar continued:

> When the Anṣār spokesman stopped, I wanted to deliver a speech which appealed to me. But Abū Bakr said: 'Gently, 'Umar.' I did not want to make him angry. So he spoke instead. He was certainly more knowledgeable and more sagacious than I. And by God, his spontaneous intuitive speech included all the wonderful thoughts that surged through my

mind either in a similar or better way. Then he was silent. Among the things which he, may God be pleased with him, said was: 'As for whatever good you mentioned about yourselves, you certainly deserve them.' He commended them and what they contributed to their religion and to their brothers in faith, the Muhājirūn. He recalled their merits and their virtues which even their own spokesmen did not mention. Then he began to disentangle the problem from the framework in which the Anṣāri spokesman had placed it. He emphasized that the matter was not limited to Madinah alone but concerned the whole Arabian peninsula—whether this whole region would continue to be under the influence of Islam. If the Muhājirūn lived in Madinah it is possible that they would have granted the succession to their Anṣārī brethren in recognition of their merits. But the rest of the Arabs would only submit to the Quraysh. And if unity was not achieved then the message of Islam would not be destined to cross boundaries and spread outside the peninsula. Thus the interests of Islamic propagation (*da'wah*) required that the succession (*khilāfah*) to the noble Prophet should be from among the Quraysh in order to carry forward the message and keep hearts together. He then requested them to choose between two people from the Quraysh whose excellence no one could doubt: 'Umar ibn al Khaṭṭāb and Abū 'Ubaydah ibn al Jarrāḥ. He himself withdrew.

'Umar is on record as having said:

> I have never disliked anything more than what was said by Abū Bakr (namely, his nomination of 'Umar and Abū 'Ubaydah). By God, it would have been more preferable to me to have my neck struck off without entailing any sin than to be a ruler over a people among whom was Abū Bakr.

Another spokesman from among the Anṣār stood up and wanted to shift the issue back into the framework suggested by the first spokesman, and proposed that there should be one ruler (*amīr*) from the Anṣār and another from the Quraysh. 'Umar described the situation then: "There was much talk and people raised their voices so loudly that I feared disagreement (would ensue). So I said: 'Give me your hand,

O Abū Bakr.' He offered me his hand and I pledged allegiance to him. Then the Muhājirūn followed suit and then the Anṣar." In the ensuing rush, Sa'd ibn 'Ubādah, the nominee of the Anṣār, may God be pleased with him, was accidentally trampled upon."[5]

In this way the Companions of the Prophet were able to settle this dispute without leaving any trace of rancor in their hearts and to unite on the primary objective of carrying forward the message of Islam.

Payment of Zakāh Controversy

The fourth serious controversy was about the legitimacy of fighting those who refused to pay the obligatory tax of zakāh after the death of the Prophet. Once again, the Companions were able to overcome this crisis through their genuine sincerity and their adherence to the ethics of disagreement.

After allegiance had been pledged to Abū Bakr as the successor (*khalīfah*) of the Prophet, some of the tribes who had recently become Muslims, renounced Islam. Some followed impostors, like Musaylamah, who claimed to be prophets. Other tribes refused to perform *ṣalāh* or pay the zakāh. Some only refused to pay the zakāh to Abū Bakr out of arrogance and conceit. Others did so because they came up with a false interpretation claiming that zakāh, according to the Sharī'ah, was originally payable only to the Prophet. They cited the following verse claiming that only the person addressed in it, namely the Prophet, had the authority to collect zakāh from them and had the ability to confer on them the benefits of purification:

> Take alms (*ṣadaqah*) from their wealth that you may purify and sanctify them; and pray on their behalf [for] indeed your prayers are a source of security for them. And God is the one who hears and knows (9: 103).

In this interpretation, those who refused to pay zakāh either forgot or ignored the fact that the address in this verse was not confined to Muḥammad as Prophet only but also as ruler and leader of the Muslims. The collection and distribution of zakāh is part of the organization and administration of Muslim society, as is the application of other laws such

5. All the above quotations in ibid., 2/656-661.

as the fixed criminal code. The responsibility for carrying out these functions devolves on those who come after the Prophet and who act on behalf of the Muslim Ummah in the capacity of rulers and leaders.

Furthermore, whenever a Muslim pledged allegiance to the Prophet, he pledged among other things to establish regular *ṣalāh* and pay zakāh – the two were and are inseparable. The first successor of the Prophet was keen on the protection and advancement of Islam and so decided to fight those who chose to withhold zakāh to make them repent and return to the fold of Islam, fully committed to abide by all that they had pledged to the Prophet.[6]

'Umar ibn al Khaṭṭāb was instinctively against the permissibility of fighting those who withheld zakāh and confronted Abū Bakr on the issue. Abū Hurayrah, may God be pleased with him, has narrated how the dispute arose and how it was finally resolved:

> When the Messenger of God, may God bless him and grant him peace, passed away, Abū Bakr succeeded him and some of the Arabs reverted to *kufr*. 'Umar said: 'How can you fight people when the Messenger of God, may God bless him and grant him peace, has said: 'I was commanded to fight people until they say 'There is no god but Allah (*lā ilāha illā Allāh*)'. And whoever utters these words, his life and his property are inviolable except that which is he liable to pay and account for to God Almighty?' Abū Bakr said: 'By God, I will certainly fight whoever makes a separation between *ṣalāh* and zakāh, for indeed zakāh is liable on wealth. By God, if they withhold from me even a little goat which they used to pay during the lifetime of the Prophet, I would fight withholding it.' 'Umar said: 'By God, it was none other than Allah Who opened Abū Bakr's heart towards this decision to fight, and I realized that he was right.'[7]

Ibn Zayd also says in this respect:

> 'Establishing *ṣalāh* and paying zakāh were prescribed together – there was no separation between the two,' and he recited the following verse: "But if they repent, establish

6. Al Bukhārī, in *Fatḥ al Bārī*'s commentary, 3/212.
7. Ibid., 3/211.

regular *ṣalāh* and pay the zakāh, they are your brethren in faith" (9: 11). That is why Abū Bakr refused to accept *ṣalāh* without zakāh. May Allah bless Abū Bakr for his clear understanding of Islam and his determination to confront those who tried to separate *ṣalāh* from zakāh.[8]

The cause of the controversy between Abū Bakr and 'Umar was that the latter adhered to the literal meaning of the ḥadīth and considered that uttering the *shahādah* was sufficient for admitting a person into the fold of Islam and making his property and his life inviolable. On the other hand, Abū Bakr insisted that this was conditional on the phrase "except that which he is liable to pay." He considered zakāh as a due or liability on wealth which must be paid if a person were to be granted inviolability of life and property. In addition, he understood that the joining of *ṣalāh* and zakāh in many verses of the Qur'an and in the sayings of the Prophet meant that these pillars were not to be separated.

Since both parties were agreed that the refusal to establish regular *ṣalāh* was evidence of apostasy as was following a false claimant to prophethood, so the refusal to pay zakāh should be considered as evidence of apostasy for which the apostates should be fought. In this way, Abū Bakr was able to convince the rest of the Companions of the soundness of his ijtihad to fight those who refused to pay zakāh,[9] to consider them apostates so long as they did not repent, establish *ṣalāh* and pay the zakāh. Thus this critical dispute was settled. The decision was vital for the preservation of Islam against the malicious attempts to demolish it pillar by pillar after the attempts to demolish it in one go had failed. Had it not been for this courageous and unflinching stand by Abū Bakr and the subsequent support from the companions, Islam would not have remained intact, or it would have been confined to Makkah and Madinah, and apostasy and civil strife would have dominated the entire Arabian peninsula.[10]

Juristic Issues

If we leave aside these serious matters which were brought under

---

8. Al Ṭabarī, *Tafsīr*, 10/62.

9. For a detailed discussion of the debate between Abū Bakr and 'Umar and the comments of scholars on this issue, see *Nayl al Awṭār*, 4/175 ff.

10. For further details, see for example *al Bidāyah wa al Nihāyah*, 6/311 ff.

control and examine other issues, we will find some remarkable examples of adherence to the ethics of disagreement and mutual respect among the *'ulamā'* in the community. Among the matters which the "two venerable leaders"–Abū Bakr and 'Umar–differed on was the question of prisoners of war, the distribution of liberated lands, and the equality of financial provision for Muslims.

As regards female prisoners of war, Abū Bakr was of the opinion that they should be kept under Muslim custody. But during his *khilāfah*, 'Umar revoked this decision and set the female prisoners of war free and allowed them to go back to their families, apart from those who had children from the men to whom they were entrusted. As regards liberated lands, Abū Bakr distributed them but 'Umar retained them in the state's control as trusts or endowments (*waqf*). Regarding financial provision for Muslims, Abū Bakr maintained that there should be equality in stipends while 'Umar opted for preferential treatment for various categories of Muslims.

On the question of succession, we may note that 'Umar did not nominate anyone as his successor while Abū Bakr himself nominated 'Umar as his successor. They also had various differences about many juristic issues.[11] But these differences only increased their love for one another as brothers in faith. When, for example, Abū Bakr nominated 'Umar as his successor, some Muslims asked him: "What would you say to your Lord and Sustainer when He asks you about your nomination of 'Umar over us although you know of his harshness?" Abū Bakr replied: "I would say: 'O Lord, I have nominated as my successor the best of Your adherents.'"[12] And when one of the Muslims told 'Umar, may God be pleased with him: "You are better than Abū Bakr," 'Umar wept and said: "By God, one night of Abū Bakr's life is better than [the life of] 'Umar and his family."[13]

These are examples of differences between these two men of great wisdom and stature. Their opinions differed but not their hearts, because they looked up to heaven and God's pleasure and not down to earthly power.

'Umar and 'Alī

There were differences of opinion between 'Umar ibn al Khaṭṭāb

11. See Ibn Ḥazm, *al Iḥkām*, 6/76.
12. See Ibn Sa'd, *Ṭabaqāt*, 3/199, and *al Kāmil*, 2/292.
13. See *Ḥayāt al Ṣaḥābah*, 1/646.

and 'Alī ibn Abī Ṭālib, but these were kept within the bounds of refined manners. The following story demonstrates this:

> There was a woman whose husband was away. 'Umar, who was then the *khalīfah*, was told that she admitted men into her house in the absence of her husband. As 'Umar disapproved of this, he sent someone to summon her to him. "Go to 'Umar," she was told and she said: "Oh, woe unto me! Why should 'Umar want to see me?" The woman was pregnant, and on her way to him she was so scared that she went into labor. She therefore entered a house where she gave birth to a child who died shortly afterwards. 'Umar consulted the Companions of the Prophet, some of whom advised that he was not to be blamed for anything; he was only doing what his office required of him. 'Alī, on the other hand, kept silent. Noticing that, 'Umar came up to 'Alī and asked him: "What do you say?" 'Alī replied: "If what these Companions said is what they really think, then their opinion is wrong. But if they said that in order to please you, they have not given you proper advice. I believe that you have to pay compensation (*dīyah*) for the child. It is you who scared the woman, and she miscarried because of you."[14]

'Umar yielded to the opinion of 'Alī without feeling any resentment in acting on his verdict, even though he was the head of the Muslim state (*amīr al mu'minīn*). He felt a certain relief in following the opinion of another.

'Umar and 'Abd Allāh ibn Mas'ūd

'Abd Allah ibn Mas'ūd was one of the most well-versed of the Prophet's Companions in the Qur'ān and one of the most knowledgeable in the Sunnah of the Prophet. Many of the Companions even regarded him as part of the Prophet's household, so close was he to the Prophet. Abū Mūsā al Ash'arī has said: "There was a time when we used to think that 'Abd Allāh ibn Mas'ūd and his mother were relatives of the Prophet because of their closeness to him and because they were often seen fre-

14. Transmitted by Muslim, Abū Dāwūd, al Nasā'ī, Ibn Ḥibbān and others.

quenting his house. One day when Abū Mas'ūd al Badrī saw 'Abd Allāh ibn Mas'ūd approaching, he pointed at him and said: "The Prophet has not left behind anybody more knowledgeable of the divine revelation than that man who is approaching." Abū Mūsā said: "This man used to be present with the Prophet when we were away and he used to give us permission to meet the Prophet when we waited outside."[15]

'Umar was well-known for his profound understanding of Islam and his great abilities. Ibn Mas'ūd was one of the men chosen by 'Umar to perform various assignments. He concurred with 'Umar in many of his judgments, to the extent that historians of Islamic jurisprudence considered that he was more influenced by 'Umar than by any other Companion. Their methods of deduction were often similar and their juristic decisions often coincided. It is in fact likely that Ibn Mas'ūd resorted to 'Umar's conclusions on some juridical issues[16] as, for example, on some questions relating to inheritance.

However, in spite of their closeness and mutual respect for each other, 'Umar and Ibn Mas'ūd had their differences on various issues. Ibn Mas'ūd used to place his right hand over the left in *ṣalāh* but would not place them on his knees. 'Umar did the latter but did not approve of the former.

Ibn Mas'ūd was of the opinion that if a husband says to his wife: "You are unlawful to me," the utterance is equal to an oath implying irrevocable divorce. 'Umar, however, considered this as only one, not the final, pronouncement of divorce.

If a man committed sexual intercourse with a woman and then married her, Ibn Mas'ūd regarded the marriage as invalid and the man and woman as living in a state of lewdness and adultery. 'Umar, on the other hand, regarded the initial relationship as adulterous but the marriage as valid.[17]

In his book *I'lām al Muwaqqi'īn*, Ibn al Qayyim pointed out that Ibn Mas'ūd and 'Umar ibn al Khaṭṭāb differed on a hundred juristic issues, and he cited four of these.[18] Nonetheless, their differences did not lessen or weaken their love and respect for each other. This is amply illustrated by the following:

> Two men came to Ibn Mas'ūd. One of them was instructed [in reciting the Qur'an] at the hands of 'Umar ibn al Khaṭṭāb

15. Transmitted by Muslim. See Ibn Ḥazm, *al Iḥkām*, 6/63.
16. See *al Iḥkām*, 1/61.
17. Ibid.
18. Ibn al Qayyīm, *I'lām al Muwaqqi'īn*, 2/218.

> and the other was taught by another Companion. The former said: "'Umar ibn al Khaṭṭāb taught me to recite." Ibn Mas'ūd and the other was taught by another Companion. The former said: "'Umar ibn al Khaṭṭāb taught me to recite." Ibn Mas'ūd wept on hearing this and then said: "Recite as 'Umar has taught you to recite. He was indeed a fortress for Islam. Once people entered this fortress, they never left it. But when he was assassinated, the fortress started to crack."[19]

One day while 'Umar was sitting, he saw Ibn Mas'ūd coming towards him and said: "There comes a citadel full of wisdom and knowledge." In another version, 'Umar is reported to have said: "Ibn Mas'ūd is a citadel full of knowledge which would benefit the people of Qādisīyah."[20]

May God be pleased with these two men. Despite their differences of opinion on some issues, their feelings towards each other only increased in mutual respect and love. From these events, we can derive a body of ethics which can be a model in treating problems relating to disputes.

Ibn 'Abbās and Zayd ibn Thābit

To get more insight into the ethics of disagreement we could examine some specific issues over which some of the Companions differed.

Like many of the Companions of the Prophet, including Abū Bakr, Ibn 'Abbās used to think that the grandfather of a deceased person should receive the entire inheritance to the exclusion of brothers and sisters. This was on the assumption that the grandfather should be treated in the same manner as the father in inheritance. Other Companions such as Zayd ibn Thābit, 'Alī ibn Abū Ṭālib, and Ibn Mas'ūd held that the estate should be divided between the grandfather and the children of the deceased. Commenting on this view, Ibn 'Abbās is reported to have said:

> "Doesn't Zayd fear God in equating the grandson with the son while refusing to grant the grandfather the right of the father in inheritance?" And he added: "I wish that I and those

19. See *al Iḥkam* (6/61).
20. Ibn Sa'd, *Ṭabaqāt*, 4/161; *Ḥayāt al Ṣaḥābah*, 3/791.

who differ with me about inheritance matters should meet and place our hands on the corner of the Ka'bah and invoke God's wrath on those who are liars."[21]

By citing these examples of legal differences among the Companions, we do not seek to delve into or perpetuate disagreement; instead we seek to discover the norms of proper behavior which will hopefully enable us to solve our differences on legal issues, and consequently highlight the true Islamic spirit in dealing with people. Ibn 'Abbās, as we have seen, was very confident that his judgment was right and that Zayd's was wrong. Yet when Ibn 'Abbās saw Zayd riding one day, he took the reins of Zayd's mount and led him as a gesture of respect. Zayd protested saying: "Do not do that, O cousin of the Messenger of God, may God bless him and grant him peace." Ibn 'Abbās replied, "This is how we have been instructed to treat our learned ones and our elders." Zayd responded by asking for Ibn 'Abbās' hand. Zayd took the proffered hand and kissed it, saying: "This is how we have been instructed to behave towards the family (*ahl al bayt*) of our Prophet."[22] When Zayd died, Ibn 'Abbās commented: "Thus does knowledge pass away."[23] In al Bayhaqī's version, Ibn 'Abbās is reported to have said: "This is the way knowledge passes away. Today, knowledge in abundance has been buried."[24]

'Umar, may God be pleased with him, used to call upon Ibn 'Abbās to deal with problematic issues together with other learned and venerable Muslims both from among the Muhājirūn and Anṣār whose experience went back to the time of the battle of Badr.[25]

Indeed, if we try to trace the differences amongst the Companions about juristic issues and their conduct in explaining their respective positions, we could fill volumes. This of course is not our purpose here. Our intention here is only to cite some examples from which we can see the type of ethical behavior which shaped the lives of the generation of the Prophet's Companions, may God be pleased with them all. This would indicate the extent of their commitment in all circumstances to the ethics of disagreement.

For reasons only known fully to God, grave incidents of civil strife in which the Companions physically fought against each other did occur. Yet even in these dire and momentous circumstances the Compa-

21. See Ṭāhā Jābir al 'Alwānī, *al Maḥṣūl*, 2nd. ed. 5/55.
22. *Kanz al 'Ummāl*, 7/37; *Ḥayāt al Ṣaḥābah*, 3/30.
23. *I'lām al Muwaqqi'īn*, 1/18.
24. Al Bayhaqī, *Sunan*, 6/211; *al Maḥsūl*, 2nd ed. 5/56.
25. *Al Maḥṣūl*, 2nd ed. 4/154 ff.

nions never lost sight of each other's virtues and merits. Here is what Marwān ibn al Ḥakam said of 'Alī, may God be pleased with him: "I have not seen anyone more generous in victory than 'Alī. [After our defeat] in the Battle of the Camel, he was nothing but our protector. He ordered one of his men to announce that none of the wounded should be finished off."[26]

On another occasion 'Imrān ibn Ṭalḥah visited 'Alī ibn Abī Ṭālib after the Battle of the Camel was over. 'Alī welcomed him warmly, asked him to sit near him, and said: "I really hope that God will make your father and me among those whom He described: 'And We shall remove from their hearts any feeling of rancor and [they shall be] brothers [joyfully] facing each other on thrones [of dignity]'" (15: 47). Then 'Alī began asking 'Imrān about each member of his father's household, one by one. Some of those present who were not fortunate to have had the honor of the Prophet's company and who did not realize what it meant for a person to be a Companion of the Prophet were surprised at this. Two men who were seated nearby remarked: "God is more just than this. You were killing them yesterday and [now] you are brothers in Paradise!" 'Alī became angry and said to both of them: "Get up and go as far away in God's land as you can. Who is it then (who fits the description of this Qur'anic verse) if it is not Ṭalḥah and I? Who is it then?"[27]

'Alī was once asked whether those who fought against him in the Battle of the Camel were polytheists. He, may God be pleased with him, said: "From polytheism they fled." When asked whether they were hypocrites, he replied: "Hypocrites only rarely remember God." When asked what in fact they were, he replied: "They are our brothers who committed an injustice against us."[28]

Someone spoke ill of 'Ā'ishah, the Prophet's wife, in the presence of 'Ammār ibn Yāsir. Although 'Ammār did not support 'Ā'ishah during the Battle of the Camel, he was outraged and said: "Be quiet, you loud and disgraceful one! How can you be offensive to the beloved of the Prophet of God, may God bless him and grant him peace? I bear witness that she is the Prophet's wife in paradise. Our mother 'Ā'ishah took the course she chose. We know that she is the Prophet's wife in this life and the hereafter. But God made her a test for us to see whether we would obey Him or her."[29]

---

26. *Ḥayāt al Ṣaḥābah*, 3/12.
27. Ibid., 3/13; also Ibn Sa'd, *al Ṭabaqāt*, 3/224.
28. Transmitted by al Bayhaqī in *al Sunan*, 8/173.
29. Ibid. Also *Kanz al 'Ummāl*, 7/166; *Ḥayat al Ṣaḥābah*, 3/14.

What more proper behavior could one expect from people whom God willed that they should fight against each other? The light which emanated from the beacon of prophethood continued to illuminate hearts which hate could not overwhelm. Such was the lofty standard of ethics and behavior which the Companions adopted in their differences. It was not fitting that controversy and a deviation from ethical behavior should co-exist in the hearts of men of goodness.

Ibn 'Abbās Debates with the Khawārij

The discussions which took place between Ibn 'Abbās and the Khawārij are very instructive not only of the knowledge and prowess of Ibn 'Abbās, but also of his courage and determination to resolve differences and disagreements through an appeal to reason and, in the first instance, to the Qur'an and the Sunnah.

Ibn 'Abbās relates that 'Alī ibn Abi Ṭālib instructed: "Do not fight them [the Khawārij] until they secede. They will secede." Ibn 'Abbās said: "O *Amīr al Mu'minīn*! Be soothed with prayer (*ṣalāh*). I want to go to the Khawārij, listen to what they have to say and talk to them." "I am afraid for you on their account," replied 'Alī. Confident of his own peacefulness as one not known to cause anyone any harm, Ibn 'Abbās put on his best Yemeni clothes and walked to the camp of the Khawārij. "What sort of clothes are these?" they asked Ibn 'Abbās, who replied by reciting the verse of the Qur'an: 'Say! Who has declared unlawful the beautiful gifts of God which He has produced for His servants and the pure and wholesome things which He has provided for sustenance?" (7: 32) and added: "I saw the Prophet, may God bless him and grant him peace, wearing the best Yemeni clothes." "It's all right," said the Khawārij, "but what brings you here?" He replied: "I come to you from the camp of the cousin and Companion of the Prophet, may God bless him and grant him peace. The Companions of the Prophet, peace be on him, know more about the Revelation than you and it was among them that the Qur'an was revealed. I come to tell you about them and then go back and tell them about you. Why are you hostile to them?" Dismissively, one of the Khawārij said: "Beware of talking to him. The Quraysh are indeed a contentious people. God, Exalted and Glorified is He, said: 'Indeed, they are a contentious people'" (43: 58).

Another suggested that they should talk to him and they nominated two or three men to do so. They gave Ibn 'Abbās the choice of who should speak first, and he suggested that they should. The men proceeded to relate three complaints against 'Alī ibn Abī Ṭālib. The first was that he had appointed men to pass judgment in matters pertaining to the religion of God knowing that God has said: "Judgment rests with none but God" (6: 57). They referred to the fact that 'Alī had agreed to accept the arbitration of Abū Mūsā al Ash'arī and 'Amr ibn al 'Āṣ in the dispute with Mu'āwiyah. In reply Ibn 'Abbās said that God has allowed men to pass judgment in matters pertaining to His religion even in the case of a quarter dirham, a rabbit,[30] or a dispute between a man and his wife. In this latter case he cited the verse of the Qur'an: "Therefore send an arbitrator from his family and an arbitrator from her family" (4: 35). And in the end, he asked: "Now which is more important: arbitration between husband and wife or arbitration to prevent the shedding of blood and to preserve the unity of the Ummah?"

They conceded this point but then complained about the fact that 'Alī did not insist on the title of *Amīr al Mu'minīn* during the arbitration process. They asked: "Is he *Amīr al Mu'minīn* or *Amīr al Kāfirīn* (Head of the Disbelievers)?" Ibn 'Abbās asked whether they would reconsider their position if he cited verses from the Qur'an and the Sunnah of the Prophet. They said they would and he continued: "You must have heard directly or indirectly that on the day of Ḥudaybīyah, Suhayl ibn 'Amr came [as a negotiator] to the Prophet, peace be upon him. The Prophet directed 'Alī: 'Write: This is the truce agreed upon by Muḥammad, the Messenger of God.' 'Amr objected saying: 'If we knew that you were the Messenger of God, we would not have fought against you.' The Prophet thereupon instructed 'Alī: 'Erase it, 'Alī.' If the Prophet did not insist on being called Messenger of God, why could 'Alī not forgo being called *Amīr al Mu'minīn*?'" They were satisfied on this point also.

Their third complaint was that 'Alī fought in the battles of Ṣiffīn and the Camel and did not take booty or prisoners of war. Ibn 'Abbās asked them: "Would you take your mother [referring to 'Ā'ishah, the wife of the Prophet] as a prisoner of war and confiscate her property? If your answer is yes, then you would be disbelievers in the Book of God and you would have left Islam . . ." Ibn 'Abbās again asked, after quoting from the Qur'an and the Sunnah, whether they were satisfied on this point and they agreed. As a result of this verbal challenge, a substantial number of the Khawārij returned to 'Alī's camp, but the majority remained

30. Ibn 'Abbās refers here to the Qur'ānic verse (5: 95) concerning the hunting of game while in a state of *iḥrām* during ḥajj.

obdurate.[31] These were people who had unsheathed their swords, and were ready to fight those who had differed from their line of thought, considering it lawful to take their lives and property. Nonetheless, when they were challenged to debate and accept the truth, many of them responded. When they were reminded of the Qur'an they reflected on it. When they were invited to dialogue they responded with open hearts. It is pertinent to ask how Muslims of the present day stand in relation to such attitudes.

'Ali and Mu'āwiyah

It is reported that Mu'āwiyah ibn Abī Sufyān asked Ḍirār ibn Ḍamrah al Kinānī to describe for him the character and demeanor of his adversary, 'Alī ibn Abī Ṭālib. Ḍirār requested to be excused but Mu'āwiyah insisted. Ḍirār then said:

> By God, 'Alī is far-sighted and dynamic. What he says is decisive and his judgment is just. Knowledge and wisdom spring from his lips and are reflected in his actions. He shows no particular liking for the world and its adornments and finds company in the night and its darkness. By God, he was tender-hearted and was wont to weep profusely. He would engage in deep thought while wringing his hands and talking to himself. He preferred clothes that were just adequate and food that was simple. He was, by God, like one of us. When we visited him he would draw us close to him, and if we asked him for help he would respond willingly. In spite of our closeness to each other we would hesitate to speak to him out of awe and reverence. He had a generous smile, dazzling like a string of pearls. He respected the pious and loved the poor. The strong would not find in him encouragement for any excesses and the weak would not despair of his justice. I bear witness by God that on many occasions in the middle of the night I saw him swaying from side to side in his *miḥrāb* (prayer niche) holding his beard, in a disturbed and restless state, and weeping like a bereaved person. Even now, it is as if I hear him saying: 'Our Lord and Sustainer! Our

31. Ibn al Qayyim, op. cit., 1/214-5.

> Lord and Sustainer!' while beseeching Him. And to the life of this world he says: 'Do you display yourself to me? Do you look out expectantly for me? Vanish from my sight. Entice someone other than me. I have relinquished you irrevocably. Your life-span is short, your company is wretched, and your temptation is easy to fall into. Ah! Ah! How little is the provision, how far away is the destination, and how desolate is the way . . .'

In spite of himself, the tears trickled down Mu'āwiyah's beard as he heard this account. As he wiped his beard with the palm of his hand, those who were present also wept bitterly. Mu'āwiyah remarked: "Such was Abū al Ḥasan, may God have mercy on him. Tell us of your grief for him, O Ḍirār." "My grief (for 'Alī) is like the grief of a mother whose only child is slain on her lap. Her tears will never dry up and her grief will never subside." Saying this, Ḍirār stood up and departed.[32]

Ethics in the Pursuit of Truth

From our treatment of controversial issues, we note that selfish desires did not motivate any of the Companions; the pursuit of truth was the distinguishing factor in the differences which arose. In the period after the Prophet's death and the end of revelation, the following norms guided the Companions:

1. They strenuously strove to avoid differences as far as possible.
2. When differences of opinion were inevitable owing, for example, to evidence being available to some and not to others or to differences in the understanding of a text or an expression, they would remain firmly within the bounds of what is allowed in striving to reach the truth. They would admit their errors without any bitterness or embarrassment while always having a tremendous respect for people of virtue, knowledge, and understanding. No one would overestimate himself or disparage the ability or the rights of his brother Muslim. The

32. *Al Ḥilyah*, 1/84.

search for truth and for the correct judgment was their mutual endeavor, and they willingly accepted the truth from whichever quarter it came.

3. They regarded the brotherhood of Islam as one of the most important principles of the religion, and without which it would be impossible to establish Islam. This brotherhood transcended differences of opinion or compromise on questions which were open to varying interpretations.
4. Matters relating to the tenets of Islamic belief were not the subject of disputation. Differences of opinion were therefore confined to subsidiary matters.
5. Prior to the *khilāfah* of 'Uthmān ibn 'Affān, may God be pleased with him, most of the Companions resided in Madinah and a few in Makkah. They rarely left their homes except for jihād and such purposes. In this way, they were able to meet frequently, consult one another and reach consensus on many matters.
6. The reciters of the Qur'ān and the *fuqahā'* were prominent and had a high standing in society. They were treated in a manner similar to the leaders of the state. Each was given due recognition in his own special field. They were all aware of the juristic standpoint of others and were clear about each other's methods of deduction to the extent that there existed a certain implicit understanding and agreement among them.
7. They regarded corrections of one another's judgments as a form of assistance which a person extended to his brother in faith. Such correction was not seen as exposing a fault or as a form of censure.

Chapter Five

The Historical Context (3)

The Second Generation

When 'Umar ibn al Khaṭṭāb was the head of the Muslim state, his policy was to make the Companions of the Prophet—both the Muhājirūn and the *Anṣār*—reside in Madinah. They were only allowed to go outside the city if it was necessary for them to travel, to go on an expedition or educational assignment, to take up an administrative or judicial post, or to undertake some other special task. When they had completed their tasks or tours of duty, they had to return to Madinah—the nerve center of the Muslim state and the seat of the *khilāfah*—to take up permanent residence. In their capacity as bearers of the message of Islam and the first line of support for the *khalīfah*, they had to remain close to him to assist him in his various tasks and to participate fully in all the affairs of the Ummah.

When 'Uthmān succeeded 'Umar, he did not see any problem in allowing the Companions to leave Madinah and reside permanently wherever they liked in the Muslim lands. As a result, the jurists and reciters of the Qur'an among them spread out into the towns of the newly liberated lands and into the areas which became garrison towns. It is estimated that more than three hundred Companions settled in the garrison towns of Basrah and Kufah, and that a large number of them moved to Egypt and Greater Syria.

It is reported that when the Prophet, peace be on him, returned from the campaign of Ḥunayn (8 AH/13 AC), there were 12,000 Companions in Madinah. At the time of the Prophet's death, there were 10,000 of these Companions in Madinah while 2,000 had moved to other towns.[1]

In the Tradition of the Companions

The knowledge of the jurists and reciters of the Qur'an among the

1. *Al Fikr al Sāmī*, 1/311.

Companions was transmitted by them directly to the next generation—the Tābi'ūn or Successors. Among these were Sa'īd ibn al Musayyib,[2] who was considered as the transmitter of the legacy of 'Umar ibn al Khaṭṭāb and the upholder of his jurisprudence in Madinah; 'Aṭā' ibn Abū Rabāḥ in Makkah, Ṭāwūs in the Yemen, Yaḥyā ibn Abī Kathīr in Yamāmah, al Ḥasan in Basrah, Makḥūl in Syria, 'Aṭā' in Khurasān, 'Alqamah in Kufah, and others. These Tābi'ūn used to make juristic decisions and exercise ijtihād in the presence of the Companions of the Prophet from whom they had received knowledge and training. They were conditioned by the ethics and high standards of the Companions' behavior and influenced by their methods of juristic inference and deduction. On occasions when the Tābi'ūn differed, they did not deviate from or transgress the ethical standards of behavior set by the Companions. Jurists from this generation were to have a great influence on the masses of the Ummah, and it was through them that the knowledge and discipline of jurisprudence were transmitted. The following debates on compensation would perhaps illustrate the ethical standards of behavior which they followed.

It is reported[3] that a man came to Shurayḥ and asked what was the compensation for the loss of fingers. Shurayḥ replied that ten camels was the compensation for each finger. The man exclaimed: "Good God! Are this and this equal (pointing to his little finger and his thumb)?" "Woe to you!" said Shurayḥ. "The Sunnah prohibits such analogical deduction (*qiyās*). Follow and do not innovate." In so saying, he no doubt perceived an unwarranted extension of the Sunnah.

Mālik in his *al Muwaṭṭā'* reported that Rabī'ah said:

> I asked Sa'īd ibn al Musayyib how much compensation was payable for the loss of a woman's finger. "Ten camels," he replied. I asked him what was the compensation for two fingers. "Twenty camels," he replied. "And for three fingers?" "Thirty camels," he replied. "And for four fingers? "Twenty camels," he replied. I asked (incredulously): "Does compensation payable to a woman decrease when her injury is greater and her affliction is more severe?" Here Sa'īd asked: "Are you

2. Sa'īd ibn al Musayyib was regarded as the most distinguished scholar among the second generation of Muslims—the Tābi'ūn. He was born in 15 AH and died in 94 AH. There are several biographical sketches of him, for example, in: Ibn Sa'd, *al Ṭabaqāt al Kubrā*, 5/119-123; *Tahdhīb al Tahdhīb*, 4/84; *al Bidāyah*, 9/99.

3. In *Al Fikr al Sāmī*, 1/391 and other sources.

> an Iraqi?" Rabīah replied: "Rather think of me as a jurist well-grounded in knowledge or as an ignorant person who desires to be better instructed." Sa'īd replied: "Son of my brother, this is the Sunnah."[4]

The discussion ended then and there without either person accusing the other of ignorance or claiming that he himself was right and the other wrong. Sa'īd's judgment and that of the people of the Hijaz is based on the principle that compensation for a woman is the same as that for a man, but only up to a third of the man's compensation. Thereafter, it is half that of a man's. This is based on a ḥadīth reported by 'Amr ibn Shu'ayb. The judgment of people from Iraq, on the other hand, is that from the outset a woman's compensation is half that of a man.[5]

Another example which we may cite in this context is the argument al Sha'bī had with another person over *qiyās*. Al Sha'bī said:

> "Suppose that al Aḥnaf ibn Qays and his young son were both killed. Would the compensation for each of them be the same, or would that of al Aḥnaf be more on account of his intelligence and wisdom?" "The same, of course," replied the man. "*Qiyās* is therefore irrelevant," concluded al Sha'bī.

Al Awzā'ī met Abū Ḥanīfah in Makkah and observed:

> "Why do you not raise your hands just before *rukū'* and after?" Abū Ḥanīfah replied: "There is no recorded word or action of the Messenger of God, may God bless him and grant him peace, to authenticate this." "How so," replied al Awzā'ī, "when al Zuhrī has reported this to me on the authority of Sālim and that of his father who said that the Prophet used to raise his hands at the beginning of the *ṣalāh* and before and after *rukū'*?"

Abū Ḥanīfah also reported:

> "Ḥammād related to me through Ibrāhīm, through 'Alqamah, through al Aswad, and through Ibn Mas'ūd that the Messenger

---

4. In al Zamrānī's commentary of Mālik's *Muwaṭṭā'*, 4/188; the *Muṣannaf* of 'Abd al Razzāq, 9/349; and in al Bayhaqī, *al Sunan*, 8/96.

5. Transmitted by al Nasā'ī, 8/54; and by al Dāraquṭnī, 4/364.

of God, may God bless him and grant him peace, only raised his hands at the beginning of the *ṣalāh* and did not repeat this action again."

Al Awzā'ī then suggested that his authorities were more reliable than those of Abū Ḥanīfah, who countered:

"Ḥammād was more knowledgeable than al Zuhrī, and Ibrāhīm was more knowledgeable than Sālim. 'Alqamah was not below Ibn 'Umar in rank. And if Ibn 'Umar is to be credited as a companion of the Prophet, then al Aswad has many merits. And the merits of 'Abd Allāh ibn Mas'ūd speak for themselves." At this, al Awzā'ī remained silent.[6]

Abū Ḥanīfah is reported to have said:

"Ours is no more than an opinion. We do not oblige or coerce anyone into accepting it. Whoever has a better judgment, let him advance it."[7]

We can thus see that all Muslims were followers and upholders of the Sunnah. When the Sunnah was authenticated, no one deviated from it. If differences occurred it was only because of varying understanding or interpretation. However, when this happened each person accepted the other's point of view so long as the interpretation could be sustained by the text and there was no other authentic evidence to the contrary.

The Effect of Political Disagreement on Credal and Juristic Differences

It is important to point out that the differences which existed among the vast majority of Muslims in the early stages were in the main limited to juristic issues. These were easily resolved when they were referred to the paramount authority of texts from the Qur'an and the Sunnah Everyone imbued with the behavioral pattern of the noble Prophet yielded willingly to the truth when it was made clear to them.

---

6. *Al Fikr al Sāmī*, 1/320.
7. *Al Intiqā'*, 140.

As mentioned previously, the differences that existed were mainly due to the availability of a text to one party and the ignorance of the other party about it. They were also caused by the fact that certain texts and expressions were open to more than one interpretation.

Eventually, however, new situations arose. Political schisms emerged in the wake of the assassination of the third *khalīfah*, 'Uthmān ibn 'Affān, the transfer of the seat of government first to Kufah and then to Damascus, and the occurrence of many other upheavals. Many alien notions and developments filtered into the accepted framework for dealing with differences. A narrowness of vision and feelings of exclusiveness were encouraged whereby Muslims in each region or town began to cling to what was available to them of the Prophet's Sunnah and to view what was available to other regions with considerable caution. Their attitudes were greatly influenced by considerations of political support or opposition. As a result Iraq, with its two great garrison towns of Kufah and Basrah, became a fertile ground for the interplay of political ideas and beliefs which were disseminated to various other regions. From Iraq emerged the Shī'ah,[8] the Jahmīyah,[9] the Mu'tazilah,[10] the

---

8. The word "Shī'ah" literally means "sect" or "party." The Shī'ah are so called because of their "partisanship" for 'Alī and his descendants and the belief that they were entitled to the *khilāfah* after the Prophet, peace be on him. They also regard the leadership (*imāmah*) of the Ummah as a divine commission just as the prophethood was; the *imāmah* therefore could not be conferred through elections, nominations, or other such processes. They also believe that the *a'immah* are capable of performing miracles and that, like the prophets, they are protected from sin. There are subsects within the Shī'ah such as the Imāmīyah and the Zaydīyah, the latter being closer to the Sunnah in their beliefs than other groups. For further references on the Shī'ah consult the book *Uṣūl al Kāfī* on which there are several commentaries; Al Shahrastāni, *Al Milal wa al Niḥal*, 1/234; *I'tiqādāt Firaq al Muslimīn* (Beliefs of Muslim Sects) 77-95, published by Maktabat al Kullīyāt al Azharīyah.

9. The Jahmīyah was a sect named after Jahm ibn Ṣafwān who was killed in 128 AH. They believed that it was sacrilegious to describe God by any epithet which can be applied to others; that man has no choice or free will and that all his actions are determined by God; that Paradise and Hell will completely disappear as soon as people enter them; and that the whole of creation will disappear. References for further reading: *I'tiqādāt Firaq al Muslimīn*, 103; *Al Tabṣīr fī al Dīn*, 107-8.

10. The Mu'tazilah is the name by which this sect is most widely known, but they call themselves the "Upholders of Justice (*'Adl*) and Monotheism (*Tawḥīd*)." Their main beliefs are that nothing existed before Allah who himself is without a beginning or end, that God's attributes are not unique but have a quality of their own, and that the Qur'ān is the created, and not the eternal, word of God. See Fārūqī & Fārūqi, *The Cultural*

Khawārij[11] and a number of innovators and idiosyncratic groups. So began the fabrication of ḥadīth, the invention and circulation of political and factional stories, and the surfacing of mutual animosity and discord among people. So rife was this situation that Imām Mālik described Kufah as "the home of strife,"[12] and al Zuhrī said: "A ḥadīth which leaves us as a hand-span in length becomes an arm's length when it reaches Iraq."[13]

Keen on safeguarding their religion against innovation, heretical tendencies and corruption, Iraqi jurists themselves began taking precautions and establishing conditions, which their predecessors had not paid attention to, for the acceptance of reports concerning the Sunnah. If the Iraqis themselves were so alarmed, Muslims in other regions were even more so. The people of the Hijaz, for example, considered any hadith reported by people from Iraq and even from Syria as unacceptable unless it had some origin in their own literature.

This was why a jurist from the Hijaz, when asked about the *isnād* (chain of reporters) of a ḥadīth which the Iraqis believed to be most reliable, said that he would not accept it unless there was evidence for it in the Hijaz literature.[14]

Al 'Abbās appointed Rabī'ah ibn Abī 'Abd al Raḥmān[15] from Madinah as a minister and a consultant. After a short period Rabī'ah was discharged and returned to Madinah. When asked what he thought of Iraq and its people, he replied:

> "I saw a people who prohibit what we regard as lawful and who make lawful what we prohibit. When I left, there were

Atlas of Islam, 286-93; *al Tabṣīr fī al Dīn*, 63ff., *al Milal wa al Niḥal*, 1/61-132; *al Farq bayna al Firaq*, 93-190; *I'tiqādāt Firaq al Muslimīn*, 23ff.

11. The Khawārij or 'Seceders" from both the camps of the *Khalīfah* 'Alī ibn Abī Ṭālib and Mu'āwiyah ibn Abī Sufyān following the attempt to arbitrate between them. They eventually evolved into many subsects and developed some distinctive beliefs. One of their main beliefs is that if a believer sins he commits unbelief and becomes a *kāfir*, an outlaw, and an apostate whom it is legitimate and imperative to fight. Consequently they accused many Companions of the Prophet of unbelief such as 'Uthmān, 'Alī, Ṭalḥah, al Zubayr, and 'Ā'ishah. References for further reading: *I'tiqādāt Firaq al Muslimīn*, 51ff, *al Tabṣīr fī al Dīn*, 45 ff; *al Milal wa al Niḥal*, 1/195-256; *al Farq bayna al Firaq*, 54-93; Fārūqī & Fārūqī, *The Cultural Atlas of Islam*, p. 286.

12. *Al Fikr al Sāmī*, 1/313.

13. *Al Intiqā'.*

14. *Al Fikr al Sāmī*, 1/312.

15. Rabī'ah ibn Abī 'Abd al Raḥmān (d. circa 136 AH) was known as a master of reasoning and was one of the prominent teachers of Imam Mālik.

more than forty thousand people who were conspiring against this religion." He is also reported to have said: "It seems that the Prophet who was sent to us was different from the one sent to them!"[16]

Although these statements were aimed at the deviators and innovators in Iraq and not at the upholders of the Sunnah and the generality of the people, they do point quite clearly to some of the matters which had a far-reaching effect on the development of jurisprudence and on the attitudes of the jurists in the two regions and their methods of deduction.

Ḥijāzī and Iraqi Scholars

People of the Hijaz believed that they observed the Sunnah strictly and did not deviate from it at all. There were ten thousand companions whom the Prophet left in Madinah after the battle of Ḥunayn. They lived there till his death. 'Umar ibn 'Abd al 'Azīz used to write to the inhabitants of the garrison towns instructing them in the Prophet's Sunnah and in jurisprudence. When he wrote to Madinah, however, he would ask them about events in the city and would also request them to instruct him in the Sunnah of the Prophet so that he could disseminate it among others. Sa'īd ibn al Musayyib was well known as the upholder of the Prophet's Sunnah and the established methods and practice of the Companions in Madinah. He and the other *'ulamā'* among his contemporaries in Madinah—from among the Tābi'ūn—were of the opinion that what was available to them of the Sunnah and established practice was sufficient to meet the needs of jurisprudence. They believed that there was nothing to induce them to adopt juristic reasoning with all its snares. However, there were other jurists who differed with them and adopted juristic reasoning to such an extent that they were known as "the people of juristic reasoning (*ahl al ra'y*)". One such person was Rabī'ah ibn Abī 'Abd al Raḥmān, the teacher of Mālik, who became known as Rabī'ah the master of reasoning (*Rabī'ah al Ra'y*). The majority of Madinan jurists, however, were scholars who upheld the Sunnah and established practice.

---

16. *Al Fikr al Sāmī*, 1/312.

Iraqi scholars on the other hand, like Ibrāhīm al Nakha'ī[17] and his colleagues, believed that their share of the Sunnah was not negligible. There lived among them more than 300 highly knowledgeable companions, many of whom were jurists. At their forefront was 'Abd Allāh ibn Mas'ūd, who was among the companions who had the best understanding of the Qur'an. 'Alī ibn Abī Ṭālib also lived among them during the period of his *khilāfah*. Other prominent companions there were Abū Mūsā al Ash'arī and 'Ammār ibn Yāsir.

Ibrāhīm al Nakha'ī and the majority of Iraqi scholars held that the Sharī'ah laws were intelligible and logical; that they embodied whatever was good for public welfare; that they were based on clear unequivocal principles as well as underlying reasons or *ratio legis ('ilal*; sing: *'illah*); that they were linked to considerations of public interest; that these principles and reasons could be derived from the Qur'an and the Sunnah; and that subsidiary laws could be formulated in accordance with these reasons or *ratio legis*. Hence, they argued that the competent jurist could discover the effective reasoning behind these laws and comprehend their purposes or intent. They also argued that legal texts are finite but that circumstances are not. Since revelation and the clear textual rulings (*nuṣūṣ*) came to an end with the Prophet's death, it would be impossible to meet the needs of legislation unless the underlying reasons for particular rulings derived from the Qur'an and the Sunnah were determined and acted upon.

It is fitting to recall here that Ibrāhīm al Nakha'ī was asked by al Ḥasan ibn 'Ubayd Allāh al Nakha'ī whether he based all his juristic judgments on precedents he had heard. He replied in the negative and al Ḥasan, apparently surprised, then asked him: "Do you pass judgment on the basis of what you have not heard?" Ibrāhīm replied: "[There are precedents which] I have heard. But when faced with an issue on which I have not heard anything, I apply analogical deduction using what I have heard."[18]

This in fact was a feature of the Iraqi school of jurisprudence; they would rely on reason in the absence of a precedent (*athar*) from the Companions of the Prophet.

---

17. Ibrāhīm al Nakha'ī (d. 96 AH) was considered head of the school of reasoning (*al ra'y*). He inherited the jurisprudence (fiqh) of Ibn Mas'ūd and is regarded as very trustworthy. He is credited with having brought fiqh and ḥadīth together. When he died, Al Sha'bī said: "Ibrāhīm has not left behind anyone like himself."

18. *Al Faqīh wa al Mutafaqqih*, 1/203.

On the other hand, Sa'īd ibn al Musayyib together with other scholars from Madinah did not pay much attention to the reasons behind any law in making rulings except when indicated by a particular text or precedent. He felt he was in a position to do so inasmuch as he said: "There is no judgment passed by the Prophet, may God bless him and grant him peace, or by Abū Bakr, 'Umar, 'Uthmān, or 'Alī that I do not know of."[19] Furthermore, the society in Madinah did not experience the changes nor was it beset by the upheavals that occurred in Iraq. This is why when many a scholar from Madinah was consulted about a particular issue, he would reply if he had a precedent or tradition to follow. If not, he would decline to give an answer. Masrūq was asked about a certain issue and answered: "I do not know." He was then asked to apply analogy to reach a judgment and he said: "I am afraid that I may slip."[20]

The fear which the people of Madinah had of applying independent reasoning on issues on which no precedent or tradition was available can be clearly seen in the statement of Ibn Wahb. He reported that Mālik said:

> The Prophet, may God bless him and grant him peace, was both the leader (imām) of the Muslims and the most learned person of all. Nonetheless if he was asked about something [he was not sure of], he would not reply until the answer was revealed to him by God. If the Messenger of the Lord and Sustainer of the worlds only replied on the basis of revelation, how supremely insolent or dangerously risky it is for someone to reply on the basis of independent reasoning, analogy, blind imitation of an allegedly good person, custom, convention, politics, tact, visionary experience, dreams, preference, or conjecture. We seek help from God and in Him we trust.[21]

Although the controversy between the two schools of thought was intense and criticism vigorously exchanged, neither side forsook the ethics and proper standards of behavior in their disagreement, as was clearly seen in the conduct of debates we have described and in many others

---

19. Ibn Sa'd, *al Ṭabaqāt*.
20. Ibn Ḥazm, *I'lām al Muwaqqi'īn*, 1/257.
21. Ibid, 1/256.

which the scholars from both schools engaged in.[22] None of them crossed the limits of proper behavior by making pronouncements of unbelief and immorality, or accusations of sinful innovation or downright exclusion from the fold of Islam.

Ibn Abī Shabramah related that he and Abū Ḥanīfah visited his friend Ja'far ibn Muḥammad ibn al-Ḥanafīyah. He greeted Ja'far and introduced Abū Ḥanīfah saying: "This man is from Iraq. He is a man of understanding and intelligence." Ja'far said: "Is he perhaps the one who uses analogy and independent reasoning in religious matters? Is he al Nu'mān?" Abū Ḥanīfah replied: "Yes, may God improve you and make you prosper." Ja'far then said: "Be conscious of God and do not use analogy and independent reasoning in religious matters. *Iblīs* (Satan) was the first to use analogy to justify his disobedience of God's command to prostrate to Adam when he said: 'I am better than he. You created me from fire and You created him from clay.'" The following exchange then took place:

> Ja'far: Tell me about a statement whose beginning is unbelief and whose end is faith.
>
> Abū Ḥanīfah: I do not know.
>
> Ja'far: The statement is, 'There is no god but Allah.' If a person says the first part, 'There is no god' and stopped there, he would be a disbeliever . . . Now—woe to you!—which is more heinous in the sight of God: Murder, which God has forbidden, or adultery?
>
> Abū Ḥanīfah: Murder, of course.
>
> But Ja'far said: God requires two witnesses to prove the crime of murder but would only accept four to prove adultery. So how can you apply analogy here? He then asked: Which is greater—fasting (*ṣawm*) or prayer (ṣalāh)?
>
> Abū Ḥanīfah: Prayer, of course.
>
> Ja'far: How is it then that a woman must make up for the days of fasting she misses during menstruation but does not have to make up for the *ṣalāh* the misses? Fear Allah, O servant

22. Ibid, 1/130 ff.

> of God, and do not use analogy. We will all one day, you and I, stand before God. We will say, 'God, Glorified and Exalted is He, has said and the Prophet, may God bless him and grant him peace, has said . . .' while you and your companions will say, 'We applied analogy and used independent reasoning.' And God will do with both you and us as He wishes."[23]

The questions raised by Imam Ja'far were not too difficult for someone like Abū Ḥanīfah to answer. But he chose to remain silent and not to argue out of respect for and in consideration of the proper manner in treating a descendant of the Prophet's household, as Ja'far was.

These exchanges and debates show that the sublime ethics and norms of behavior set by the noble Prophet greatly influenced those who were involved. They also show that differences in methodology and opinion did not result in estrangement and the setting up of barriers between brothers in faith. The coarse harshness which historians associate with this period was in the main connected with groups of scholastic theologians who extended their differences to matters of belief. Some felt themselves justified in accusing others of unbelief (*kufr*), immorality (*fisq*) or innovation (*bid'ah*). However, even among these groups history will not fail to find some norms of proper behavior to record.

23. Ibid, 1/255-6.

Chapter Six

Juristic Perspectives

Schools of Jurisprudence (*Madhāhib*)

After the age of the Companions of the Prophet and their eminent successors—in the period from the end of the first century after the hijrah to the middle of the third century—there appeared some thirteen schools of thought (*madhāhib*; singular, *madhhab*) in Islamic jurisprudence. They all identified with *Ahl al Sunnah* (Upholders of the Sunnah) school, which was and still is the predominant school in the Muslim world. Unfortunately, only the works of eight or nine of the leading scholars or *a'immah* of these schools have been fully or partially recorded. From these recorded works in their various forms, the juristic principles (*uṣūl*) and methodologies of the different schools have become known. These leading scholars were:

1. Abū Sa'īd al Ḥasan ibn Yasār al Baṣrī (d. 110 AH)
2. Abū Ḥanīfah al Nu'mān ibn Thābit ibn Zūṭī (d. 150 AH)
3. Al Awzā'ī Abū 'Amr 'Abd al Raḥmān ibn 'Amr ibn Muḥammad (d. 157 AH)
4. Sufyān ibn Sa'īd ibn Masrūq al Thawrī (d. 160 AH)
5. Al Layth ibn Sa'd (d. 175 AH)
6. Mālik ibn Anas al Aṣbaḥī (d. 179 AH)
7. Sūfyān ibn 'Uyaynah (d. 198 AH)
8. Muḥammad ibn Idrīs al Shāfi'ī (d. 204 AH)
9. Aḥmad ibn Muḥammad ibn Ḥanbal (d. 241 AH)

There are other *a'immah* such as Dāwūd ibn 'Alī al Iṣbahānī al Baghdādī (d. 270 AH) better known as al Ẓāhirī because of his insistence on sticking to the manifest (*ẓāhir*) or literal meaning of expressions in the Qur'an and the Sunnah; Isḥāq ibn Rāhawayh (d. 238 AH); and Abū

Thawr Ibrāhīm ibn Khālid al Kalbī (d. 240 AH). There are others whose schools of jurisprudence did not spread, or whose followers were not many, or who in fact were considered to be followers of the schools of the more well-known scholars.

However, the *a'immah* whose schools have lasted to this day, who have followers throughout the Muslim world, and whose principles and jurisprudence are still employed in assessing issues and in making legal judgments are mainly four: Abū Ḥanīfah, Mālik, al Shāfi'ī, and Aḥmad ibn Muḥammad ibn Ḥanbal.

Methodologies of the Famous Scholars (*A'immah*)

The three leading scholars—Mālik, al Shāfi'ī, and ibn Ḥanbal—are considered as jurists of ḥadīth and the established precedents of the Companions of the Prophet. Their jurisprudence was that of the people of Madinah whose knowledge they propagated. Imām Abū Ḥanīfah, however, was the inheritor of the jurisprudence of upholders of independent reasoning (*ahl al ra'y*), becoming the foremost advocate of this school in his age.

The difference which existed between the school of Sa'īd ibn al Musayyib—whose teachings were based on the jurisprudence and established precedents of the companions of the Prophet and which enjoyed the support of the Mālikīyah, the Shāfi'īyah and the Ḥanābilah—and the school of Ibrāhīm al Nakha'ī which relies on independent reasoning in the absence of established precedent— this difference was naturally passed on to whoever adopted the methodology of either school. The intensity with which this difference was maintained was reduced considerably particularly after the *khilāfah* went to the Banū 'Abbās—the 'Abbāsīyūn—in the middle of the second century. Following this shift of power, the 'Abbāsīyūn transferred some of the eminent scholars from the Hijaz to Iraq in order to spread the Sunnah among the people there. Some of these scholars were Rabī'ah ibn Abī 'Abd al Raḥmān, Yaḥyā ibn Sa'id al-'Irāqī,[1] Hishām ibn 'Urwah,[2] and Muḥammad ibn

1. Yaḥyā ibn Sa'īd (d. 198 AH) was a contemporary of Imām Mālik and one of the most distinguished authorities on ḥadīth, of which he knew a great deal by heart. He often made judgments according to the jurisprudence of Imām Abū Ḥanīfah.

2. Hishām ibn 'Urwah (d. 145 AH), one of the *Tābi'ūn*, was one of the most eminent scholars of Madinah of his time. He was trustworthy, knew many *aḥādīth* by heart, and was a competent jurist.

Isḥāq[3]. At the same time, some of the Iraqi scholars went to Madinah and studied with scholars there. Yūsuf Ya'qūb ibn Ibrāhīm[4] and Muḥammad ibn al Ḥasan[5] studied with Mālik. All this resulted in a mutual exchange of ideas between Iraq and the Hijaz. Nonetheless, we find that the three scholars—Mālik, al Shāfi'ī, and Ibn Ḥanbal—were quite similar in their methodology even though they differed in some approaches in using deduction. But the methodology of Imām Abū Ḥanīfah remained quite distinct.

Methodology of Imām Abū Ḥanīfah

The principles of Abū Ḥanīfah's methodology are summarized in his own statement:

> I first resort to the book of God to find evidence [if I am faced with an issue]. If I do not find any [reference] therein, I resort to the Sunnah of the Messenger of God, may God bless him and grant him peace, and authentic precedents from him which have been handed down by trustworthy persons. If I do not find anything in the Book of God or in the Sunnah of His Messenger, I resort to the statements of his Companions, drawing [freely] upon these as I wish. I do not go beyond this to the statements of others. If the line of enquiry descends to the rank of Ibrāhīm, al-Sha'bī, or Ibn al Musayyib, then I am entitled to endeavor to use my ijtihad in the same way as they had done.

These are the cardinal principles of Abū Ḥanīfah's *madhhab*. There are however some subsidiary or secondary principles which appear to give rise to differences with the other scholars:

---

3. Muḥammad ibn Isḥāq was from Madinah. He took up residence in Iraq and died there in 151 AH. He was an authority on military campaigns (*maghāzī*) and international relations.

4. Ya'qūb ibn Ibrāhīm (d. 182 AH) was from Baghdad. He was an outstanding student and staunch follower of Imām Abū Ḥanīfah. He was the chief judge during the *khilāfah* of al Hādī, al Mahdī, and al Rashīd.

5. Muḥammad ibn al Ḥasan (d. 189 AH) was a colleague of Abū Hanīfah and a disseminator of his jurisprudence. He was appointed by the *khalīfah* Hārūn al Rashīd as a judge at al Riqqah and al Rayy.

- The "general" (*'āmm*) expression is as categorical or definitive (*qaṭ'ī*) in its implication as the particular (*khāṣṣ*).[6]
- The practice of a Companion which is at variance with the general practice is taken only as a specific evidence for his practice.[7]
- The abundance of narrators does not improve the validity or weightiness of the evidence.
- No consideration should be given to a general proposition which is qualified by way of introducing a condition (*sharṭ*) or a qualification (*ṣifah*).
- No acceptance is given to a tradition, transmitted by a single person, which could harm public welfare.
- An obligatory command must be acted upon unless there is a constraint which prevents it.
- If the conduct of a competent narrator is at variance with what he has narrated, do what he was seen to have practiced practiced and not what he narrated.
- Priority should be given to a clear-cut analogy over the report of a single person (*khabar al wāḥid*) which is in contradiction to it.
- Juristic preference (*al istiḥsān*) should be adopted and analogy abandoned when there appears the need to do so. (*Istiḥsān* is the preference given to one rule over another because of its perceived superiority.)

---

6. These are complex issues connected with formal logic. The "general" (*'āmm*) is the term used by philosophers of law to comprehend a plurality and is sometimes used synonymously with the term *jāmī'* (plurality) and *kull* (totality).

The "particular" (*khāṣṣ*) is the term used to indicate the particularity of a kind, of a species, or of a single being, object, or term.

Jurists divided themselves into the generalists (advocating the priority of the "general" term), the particularists (advocating the priority of the "particular"), and the medianists (refusing to incline to one or the other without additional evidence). See Fārūqī & Fārūqī, op. cit., 248-9.

The term *qaṭ'ī* which literally means "categorical" or "absolute" is used to refer to the "absolute" authenticity of a text (*naṣṣ*) as for example a text of the Qur'ān or a *mutawātir ḥadīth*, or it may be used to refer to texts which are absolute in their authenticity but "speculative" (*ẓannī*) or ambiguous in its meaning.

7. For further elaboration of this and related juristic terms, see Kamālī, *The Principles of Islamic Jurisprudence*, pp. 131-43.

Abū Ḥanīfah is reported to have said: "We know that this is an opinion and it is the best we were able to produce. However, whoever comes with a better opinion, we will accept it."

Methodology of Imām Mālik

Mālik, may God be merciful to him, adopted a different approach. He is reported to have said: "How is it that whenever someone comes to us [with an argument], we abandon what Jibrīl brought to Muḥammad, God's peace and blessings be on him, and argue with him?"[8] We have already mentioned that Mālik's methodology was that of the people of the Hijaz, upholders of the school of Sa'īd ibn al Musayyib. The principles of Mālik's school of thought may be summarized thus, in order of priority:

- Reliance on the unequivocal verbatim text of the Qur'an.
- Reliance on the clear or manifest meaning when it is general.[9]
- Validation of evidence from the Qur'an of a divergent meaning *(mafhūm al mukhālafah)*.[10]
- Validation of a harmonious meaning *(mafhūm al muwāfaqah)*.[11]
- Reliance on the Qur'an's warnings or cautioning as the effective reason for avoiding anything which is an abomination or is immoral, as in the Qur'anic verse: "For verily, it is an abomination or is immoral and impious" (6: 145).

After these five principles with regard to the Qur'an, there are ten others from the Sunnah in order of priority:

---

8. *Al Fikr al Sāmī*, 1/378.

9. The Shafi'īyah and Ḥanābilah maintain that the application of the term "general" (*'āmm*) to all that it includes is speculative (*ẓannī*) as it is open to limitation and interpretation (*ta'wīl*) and, so long as there is such a possibility, it is not definitive (*qaṭ'ī*). For further clarification, see Kamālī, op. cit., pp. 136-7.

10. *Mafhūm al Mukhālafah* or "divergent meaning"–a meaning derived from the words of a Qur'ānic text in such a way that it diverges from the explicit meaning thereof.

11. *Mafhūm al Muwāfaqah* or "harmonious meaning"–an implicit meaning on which the text itself may be silent but is in harmony with the explicit meaning. For more detailed discussion of these terms and relevant examples, see Kamālī, op. cit, pp. 166-74.

- Consensus (*ijmā'*).
- *Qiyās*.
- The practice of the people of Madinah.
- *Istiḥsān* which involves setting aside an established analogy in favor of an alternative ruling which serves the ideals of justice and public interest in a better way.
- Blocking the means to evil (*sadd al dharā'i'*).
- Considerations of public interest (*al maṣāliḥ al mursalah*).
- Testimony by a Companion of the Prophet (if the chain of transmission is sound and he is an eminent Companion).
- Consideration of disputed matters where divergent evidence is strong.
- Presumption of continuity of that which is proven and the negation of that which had not existed (*istiṣḥāb*).
- Acceptance of some laws which existed before Islam.

Methodology of Imām al Shāfi'ī

The principles of the school of thought of al Shāfi'ī, may God be merciful to him, are contained in his book *al Risālah*, which is considered to be the first and most comprehensive book on the principles of Islamic jurisprudence. Al Shāfi'ī says in this book:

> The Qur'an and the Sunnah are the original sources of Islamic jurisprudence. If there is no clear evidence in these two, the legist may resort to *qiyās* from these two. If there is a ḥadīth of the Prophet whose chain of transmission is sound, no other sources shall be consulted. *Ijmā'* is more authoritative than the report of a ḥadīth transmitted by a single person. The interpretation of a ḥadīth should be based on its clearly apparent meaning. If the ḥadīth is open to various interpretations, preference should be given to the interpretation which is closest to the apparent meaning. If a number of *aḥādīth* pertaining to a special issue are equal in their import, preference should be given to the ḥadīth whose *isnād* is sound. In this respect, a ḥadīth whose *isnād* is interrupted (*munqaṭī'*) should not be consulted except those reported by Ibn al Musayyib.

> Analogy from a principle (*aṣl*) which has already been deduced from a previous principle is not admissible. There should be no question as to "why" or "how" with regard to the original source. Questions as to why should only be addressed to a subsidiary source of law. If analogical deduction from the original source proves to be sound, it should be accepted as such and as a basis for proof.[12]

Al Shāfi'ī therefore considered the Qur'an and the Sunnah as equal in formulating legislation. No condition should be imposed on a ḥadīth except its authenticity and correct chain of transmission, since it is in itself a (primary) source of law. Consequently, there should be no question as to "how" or "why" about a valid source of law. Al Shāfi''ī would not impose any condition on a ḥadīth which is "well-known" (*mashhūr*)[13] when it pertains to matters of general necessity, as does Abū Ḥanīfah. Unlike Mālik, al Shāfi'ī believes that a ḥadīth need not be in agreement with the practice of the people of Madinah. However, he rejects *ḥadīth mursal* (a ḥadīth transmitted by a Successor without indicating the Companion who reported it to him) in general, but accepts the *ḥadīth mursal* of Sa'īd ibn al Musayyib because in his case he possessed continuous chains of transmitters. Mālik, al Thawrī, and his contemporaries among the *Ahl al Ḥadīth* (those specializing in and adhering to ḥadīth) differed from al Shāfi'ī in this regard and used such *ḥadīth mursal* to refute contrary arguments.[14] Unlike the Mālikīyah and the Ḥanafīyah, al Shāfi'ī rejected *istiḥsān* as a source of Islamic law. In refutation of this principle, he wrote a book titled *Ibṭāl al Istiḥsān* ("Invalidating Juristic Preference") in which he made his famous statement: "Whoever argues from juristic preference is making himself the Lawmaker." He also rejected the formulation of laws on the principle of the "public interest" (*al maṣlaḥah al mursalah*) together with the proofs advanced to support this principle. He rejected the use of analogy that was not based on an effective cause (*'illah*) that was established and clearly manifest (in the Qur'an and Sunnah). He rejected proofs based on the practice of the people of Madinah. He was critical of the Ḥanafīyah for their non-compliance with many of the Sunnah practices, because the ḥadīth on

13. The *mashhūr* is defined as a ḥadīth which is originally reported by one, two, or more Companions from the Prophet or from another Companion but has later become well-known (*mashhūr*). It is of a lesser degree than *ḥadith mutawātir.*

14. *Al Fikr al Sāmī*, 1/399.

which they were based failed to meet some of their conditions—conditions for example such as the popularity of a ḥadīth. Finally, he did not confine himself to the ḥadīth of the people of the Hijaz as Mālik did.

These are the salient and the most important principles of al Shāfi'ī's school of thought. The differences between them and those formulated by the schools of Mālik and Abū Ḥanīfah are quite obvious.

Imām Aḥmad ibn Ḥanbal

The principles of the Ḥanbalī school of thought are extremely close to those of the Shāfi'ī school. These principles, in order of priority are:

1. When evidence is available in the texts of the Qur'an and the Sunnah, he does not consult any other source. If there is a ḥadīth which is "raised" (*marfū'*) to the level of authenticity, he does not give priority to any other source such as the practice of the people of Madinah, independent reasoning, analogy, a Companion's saying, or consensus based on the lack of knowledge of the questions in dispute.
2. If no text is available on a question, Ibn Ḥanbal resorts to the juristic judgments of the Companions. If he finds a Companion's saying which is not contested by other Companions, he adheres to this saying and gives it priority over any other practice, opinion, or analogy.
3. If there is a difference of opinion among the companions over a particular issue, he chooses the opinion which is closest to the Qur'an and the Sunnah and does not go beyond this. If it is not clear to him which opinion is closest to the Qur'an or the Sunnah, he would report the controversy in complete objectivity and abstain from making any decision.
4. He takes as an authority any ḥadīth, whether *mursal* or *da'īf* (weak), whose authenticity—in either its chain of transmission or content—is not absolutely beyond question, provided it does not clash with an established practice, a Companion's saying, or a consensus of opinion. He would give such a ḥadīth priority over analogical deduction.

5. In his opinion, analogy should only be resorted to as a source of law when there is a necessity of passing judgment on an issue which cannot be settled by referring it to any one of the above-mentioned sources and principles.
6. He would adopt the principle of *sadd al dharā'i'* (blocking the means to wrongdoing).[15]

Methodology of al Imām Dāwūd al Ẓāhirī

It is perhaps appropriate to give a brief idea of the principles and sources of the Ẓāhirī school of thought, inasmuch as it is one of the Islamic schools which still has some influence and a following among those who uphold the Sunnah. There were serious controversies between this school and that of Abū Ḥanīfah, and later Mālik, ibn Ḥanbal, and al Shāfi'ī. However, al Ẓāhirī recognised his great debt to al Shāfi'ī.

The salient feature of the Ẓāhirī school is its adherence to the outwardly manifest meanings of the texts of the Qur'an and the Sunnah. Priority is given to these meanings over any other considerations of alternative interpretation, judgment, or public interest. Followers of this school do not practice analogy and contend that it is only applicable when there is an effective cause or *ratio legis* (*'illah*) in a text that can be applied to another case which, though not covered by the language, is covered by this cause or reason in the text. This means that the existence of an *'illah* is a prerequisite for applying analogy.

They prohibit the use of *istiḥsān* and only draw upon the *ijmā'* arrived at during the time of the Companions. Unlike the Mālikīyah, the Ḥanafīyah and the Ḥanābilah, they do not use any ḥadīth which is *mursal* or *munqaṭi'.* They do not accept the validity of any laws previous to the Qur'an and they do not allow anyone to apply independent reasoning on the basis of the Qur'anic verse: "Nothing have We omitted from the Book" (6: 38). According to this, they argue that the laws are expressly stated in the original sources and that to disregard this is to transgress the limits set by God Almighty. They consider that following the rul-

15. *Dharī'ah* (pl: *dharā'i'*) refers to the means or the route which leads to a forbidden act. For example, "looking" at persons outside of marriage is a means (*dharī'ah*) which could lead to adultery. The forbidding of such looks is therefore considered as blocking (*sadd*) the means to wrongdoing or immoral and harmful acts.

ings handed down by a given school (*taqlīd*) is prohibited to the common man, as it is to the scholar, and that every adult Muslim has the responsibility of striving to learn the correct ruling by himself.

It is true to say that many of the principles which are attributed to the leading jurists do deviate from their actual statements and are not corroborated by authentic reports. These baseless principles are then adhered to and defended against any criticism or opposing view. All this gives rise to constant controversy and ultimately detracts attention from the Qur'ān and the Sunnah. This is one of the main causes of pernicious controversy which the *a'immah* themselves never intended. Latter-day Muslims have drifted far away from matters of high priority and have become engrossed in trivial matters. This accounts for the low depths to which Muslims have sunk.

Chapter Seven

Reasons for Differences

Differences of opinion on intellectual issues, and—by extension —on juristic ones as well, are natural on account of the inherent disparities in intelligence, understanding, and analytic capacity with which people are created. If we accept that this statement is valid. Then we must also accept that differences of opinion between several Companions during the time of the Prophet and the rightly-guided *Khulafā'* did occur, and these have been well documented. We would be doing a disservice to this religion if we denied this phenomenon. By the same token we do not regard an open discussion of these differences as detracting from the purity of the Islamic message or from the sincere intention of those Companions who had differences. Indeed we can say that in mentioning these differences openly we are in fact testifying to the objective reality and validity of the Islamic religion.

Natural Differences

Islam treats people on the basis that they are human beings who, because of a variety of factors, are often at variance with the naturally pure state in which they were created. What is comforting to the believer, however, is that the differences of opinion among the Companions did not spring from weakness in belief (*'aqīdah*) or any skepticism as to the truth of the Prophet's teachings. Instead, they resulted from a genuine desire to ascertain the truth through patient investigation and discover the purpose of the Lawgiver.

So long as the Prophet, may God bless him and grant him peace, was the source of these laws, we find that no disagreement lasted longer than it took to refer it to him. From what we have said above about early Muslim history, we can say that the causes of differences of opinion in most cass hinged on the inguistic and juristic interpretation of

Qur'anic texts and the interpretation of the Sunnah of the Prophet, peace be on him. There were certainly no hidden malicious motives behind these differences, much to the disappointment of the hypocrites who were bent on sowing the seeds of discord in the community. This accounts for the ease and the speed with which these differences dissipated as soon as the disputants met the Prophet or as soon as a relevant text was produced by anyone. From the Companions' attitude, we can see the soundness of the saying that one who possesses a sound natural disposition (*fiṭrah*) supports truth wherever he finds it.

It is to be expected that some differences and the reasons behind them should have been passed on from one age to another—there is no way of restricting these differences to a given period. However, with the rapid spread of Islam after the demise of the Prophet, there surfaced new and more critical issues in the Islamic sphere which have in turn contributed to the spirit of disagreement.

After the Assassination of the Third *Khalīfah*

In particular, since the assassination of the third *khalīfah*, 'Uthmān ibn 'Affān, the new regions to which Islam had spread were exposed to violent agitations. This imparted a new and completely alien dimension to the previously staid tradition of differences of opinion. The atmosphere of political agitation and uncertainty impelled people of every city and town to become more protective of whatever knowledge of the Prophet's Sunnah they had. They were wary of attempts to corrupt or fabricate traditions.

The cities of Kufah and Basrah emerged as centers of intellectual activity. They also provided a fertile ground for the exchange of political ideas and the proliferation of various sects such as the Khawārij, the Shī'ah, and the Murji'ah[1] as well as the Mu'tazilah, the Jahmīyah and other speculative and deviant groups.

At this time, there were as many intellectual and rationalist tendencies as there were groups, with each group formulating its own methods and principles for interpreting the texts of the Qur'an and the Sunnah

1. The Murji'ah or "Deferrers" is a sect which derives its name from the word *irjā'* which means postponing or deferring. They defer judgment of a sinner to God and the Day of Judgment. They consider that where there is faith, sin or wrongdoing does no harm; similarly where there is unbelief (*kufr*) right action is of no benefit. This position is contrary to accepted Islamic belief.

and for dealing with new controversies. There was a pressing need to put in place some controls for regulating the situation, for specifying the methodologies that could be used for deriving positive laws from the divine revelation, and for specifying what was allowed and what was not in the conduct of controversies.

Fortunately, the very principle of allowing differences of approach in matters of jurisprudence (fiqh) was generally accepted. These were matters of detail and required, to begin with, a highly specialized knowledge of evidence from the Qur'an and Sunnah. The word "fiqh" literally means understanding. By extension it is used to denote the particular understanding which a jurist or *faqīh* (literally 'one who understands') brings to certain issues. The word fiqh also refers to the body of knowledge, rulings, and judgments which comes from a jurist's understanding of issues in the light of clearly defined principles.

On the basis of the knowledge available to him, a jurist may pronounce a judgment which may actually conform to what the Lawgiver intends, or it may not. Whatever the outcome, he is not required to do more than exert the utmost of his intellectual effort to arrive at a judgment. It is likely that his judgment may coincide with the purpose of the Lawgiver or be as close as possible to it in essence, purpose, and effect.

Given this approach, difference of opinion was therefore regarded as legitimate provided it fulfilled two conditions:

1. Each disputant must have evidence or proof (*dalīl*) to authenticate his argument. Failure to provide such evidence would invalidate an argument.
2. The adoption of a divergent opinion should not lead to anything preposterous or false. If the opinion is manifestly false from the beginning, it should be abandoned straight away.

These two conditions illustrate the difference between *ikhtilāf*, which suggests a justifiable difference of opinion, and *khilāf*, which is more akin to discord. *Ikhtilāf* presumes that sincere intellectual effort is exerted to arrive at a judgment; on the whole it represents an objective methodology. *Khilāf* on the other hand departs from one or both conditions mentioned above. It is a manifestation of impulsiveness and obstinacy. It has no link with objectivity.

The jurists whose schools of thought were variously adopted by the Ummah as a whole adhered steadfastly to the two conditions mentioned above: providing necessary evidence to authenticate an argument and abandoning any position that was patently preposterous. Legal historians are not at all unanimous in specifying the causes of the juristic differences in that period in spite of the vast literature on the theme. The causes, nevertheless, could be attributed to three main factors: linguistic factors, factors pertaining to the transmission of ḥadīth, and factors pertaining to the principles and rules of deduction.

Linguistic Causes

A single word in a Qur'anic text or ḥadīth may have several different meanings. The word *'ayn* for example can mean an organ of sight, running water, pure gold, or a spy. If such a word is used in a context where it is difficult to say precisely what it means, even scholars (*mujtahidūn*) who try hard may give variant meanings of a word or expression which can be sustained by the text. Meanings may also be suggested which are totally at odds with the intended meaning of the word.

A case in point is the disagreement among jurists as to the true meaning of the word *qar'* in the verse: "And divorced women shall undergo, without remarrying, a period of three *qurū'*." (2: 228) The word *qar'* (plural: *qurū'*) can either mean menstruation or purity following menstruation. The actual length of the waiting-period can thus vary depending on which meaning is adopted. Some jurists from the Hijaz concluded that the waiting period should be three intervals of purity while jurists from Iraq concluded that it should be calculated on three occurrences of menstruation, which could mean a shorter waiting-period.[2]

Sometimes an expression can have both a literal and a figurative meaning. There was, however, disagreement among some scholars on whether in fact it was at all appropriate that Qur'anic expressions should have figurative meanings. Most scholars confirmed that it was appropriate while a few, like Abū Isfarāyīnī and Ibn Taymīyah, rejected such a possibility.

Those who did not agree that a Qur'anic expression might have figurative connotations argued that such connotations had no real bearing on the original usage of the word. Accordingly, the word "lion" for

2. See al Qurṭubī, *Tafsīr*, 3/113; and Ibn Qudāmah, *al Mughnī*, 9/77 ff.

example cannot be taken to mean "a brave man." They argued that the Qur'anic texts came to clarify laws and not to confuse them, as figurative interpretations would tend to do. Our purpose here is not to debate this issue. The majority of scholars, as we have said, were of the opinion that figurative connotations of Qur'anic texts were admissible. Ibn Qudāmah and other jurists in fact considered the rejection of figurative connotations as a mark of obstinacy.[3]

Nonetheless scholars, in studying Qur'anic texts, did differ in their understanding of the purpose of the Lawgiver. If a word suggested two interpretations, some scholars opted for the literal meaning and some for a figurative meaning. The word *mīzān* for example literally refers to a scale or an instrument for weighing things. Figuratively, it may have the connotation of "justice" as in the verse:

> And the firmament has He raised high, and He has set up the balance (*mīzān*) in order that you may not transgress the balance. So establish weight with justice and fall not short in the balance (55: 7-9).

In its last occurrence, the word *mīzān* above has the literal meaning of a scale used to weigh goods. In its first and second occurrences the word *mīzān* may signify "justice" (*'adl*) or balance,[4] as in the following verse as well:

> We have sent Our Messengers with all evidence of this truth and through them We bestowed revelation from on high and the balance (*mīzān*) so that mankind might behave with equity. (57: 25).

Figurative speech is also to be found in the overall context of a Qur'anic passage as in the verse:

> Children of Adam! We have sent down (*anzalnā*) on you clothes to cover your nakedness, and a thing of beauty (7: 26).

The word *anzalnā* literally means "We have sent down". Of course clothes were not "sent down" from the skies as clothes. A literal under-

---

3. See *Rawḍat al Nāẓir*, 35 (*Salafiyah* ed.).
4. Ibn Kathīr, *Tafsīr*, 4/270.

standing of *anzalnā* is therefore inadmissible. *Anzalnā* may instead be taken to mean "We have bestowed the knowledge of making or using." This meaning would fit other occurrences of the verb *anzala* in the Qur'an as when God said that "He bestowed the knowledge of making or using (*anzala*) iron" (57: 25). We cannot translate this literally as "And God sent down iron."

Another possible explanation of God "sending down clothes" is that God sent down the rain and caused plants to grow. He also created animals with wool, fur, and hair, and from these we make clothes. Hence the verse may refer to the finished product as a manifestation of God's bounty rather than the original water which He sent down and which is described elsewhere in the Qur'an as the source of every living thing.

Apart from the meanings of individual words, linguistic difficulties arose over questions of grammar. It is common knowledge that a direct imperative of a verb, for example "Do!", often indicates a command to fulfill an obligation; the negative imperative (Don't do!") indicates prohibition. These imperative forms, however, are not always used in this absolute sense.

The direct imperative form of a verb may be used, for example, to indicate a commendable course of action, offer guidance, give a warning, or convey some news. The command to "write out a deed of freedom" (24: 33) for any enslaved person requesting such a deed is taken by scholars either as an absolute command which has the aim of the abolition of slavery as a social institution or as indicating a commendable course of action. The command to the believers who give or take credit to "set it down in writing" (2: 282) is regarded as offering guidance and advice. The command addressed to those who deliberately turn away from the Prophet's message to "Do what you will" (41: 5) is generally regarded as a warning against the consequences of obstinacy.[5]

Apart from direct prohibition, the negative imperative may be used to encourage abstinence from acts which are improper or disliked, to offer guidance, or to convey some news. When God says: "So turn not your eyes [longingly] towards the worldly benefits which We have granted to some of those [that deny the truth]" (15: 88), the negative imperative "turn not your eyes" is taken to encourage abstinence from a potentially distressing attitude. And when God commands the believers: "Do not ask about matters which, if they were to be made manifest to you (in

---

5. See *al Maḥṣūl*, 2/39 ff where fifteen forms of the imperative are listed.

terms of law), might cause you hardship" (5:101), this is taken as offering guidance in avoiding undesirable curiosity.[6]

The varying ways of interpreting both positive and negative commands have contributed to differences among jurists in their approaches and in their methods of deriving laws from the texts of the Qur'an. Sometimes scholars may be at variance on the contextual use of words, even if they fully agree upon the meaning of the words. A case in point is the differences over the Qur'anic verse (2: 282) which deals with the role of the scribe and the witness in the recording of business transactions.

One interpretation, based on the reading of Ibn 'Abbās, gives the meaning of the verse as: "And let neither scribe nor witness cause harm." This interpretation takes the verb as being grammatically in the active voice: the scribe is taken to be guilty of writing something different from what had been dictated to him, and the witness guilty of giving false testimony.

Another interpretation, based on a reading of Ibn Mas'ūd, gives the meaning of the verse as: "And let neither scribe nor witness suffer harm." This interpretation takes the verb to be grammatically in the passive voice: both the scribe and the witness might have harm done to them if they were forced to write or testify at a time when it was not convenient for them to do so. Harm could also come to a scribe and a witness, for example, by being held responsible for the eventual consequences of the contract as such, or for the nonfulfillment of any of its provisions by either of the contracting parties.[7]

Those who are interested in investigating such causes for differences in opinion will find many examples in individual words and in grammatical constructions. According to these differences, a text may be regarded, for example, as either general or specific, absolute or limited, summing up or clarifying. Our brief treatment of the subject here may encourage the reader to study these fascinating linguistic roots of juristic differences in the specialized works available.[8]

---

6. Ibid., 469. Also, al Āmidī, *Iḥkām*, 2/187 (Riyadh edition).

7. See Ibn al Sayyid al Baṭlayūsī, *al Tanbīh 'alā al Asbāb Allatī Awjabat al Ikhtilāf bayna al Muslimīn* (Warning on the Causes Which Make for Disagreement among Muslims), 32-3.

8. Ibid.

Differences over Ḥadīth

Most of the juristic differences among the early scholars can be traced back to the narration of sayings attributed to the Prophet, peace be on him.

Sometimes a ḥadīth never reached a certain scholar and so he might formulate his judgment according to the explicit meaning of a Qur'anic text or another ḥadīth available to him. Alternatively, he might resort to *qiyās* from a relevant judgment made by the Prophet, or he would have recourse to the presumed continuation (*istiṣḥāb*) of a law not known to have been revoked where the circumstances were analogous. Or, he might base his judgment on the principle of not burdening people with obligations when there is no textual evidence to warrant it, or on some other accepted principle of reaching a judgment through ijtihād.

Sometimes in actual fact, a different ḥadīth from that available to one scholar would reach another scholar, and this would result in different judgments on the same issue.

At other times, a jurist may receive a ḥadīth which he considers to be defective, thus preventing him from using it for making a legal ruling. The following are some possibilities in this regard:

1. The chain of narration (*isnād*) going back to the Prophet may not be sound and may include a narrator who is obscure or untrustworthy, or whose memory is weak or defective.
2. The *isnād* may be "interrupted," that is to say the narrator did not cite the first authority who had heard the ḥadīth from the Prophet.
3. The jurist, especially in the case of a ḥadīth reported by a single narrator, may impose certain conditions for the probity of a narrator which others do not impose. His conclusions and his judgments on these particular issues may therefore differ from those of others.

The conclusions and judgments of scholars also differed according to their individual conceptions and definitions of the actual text and implications of certain ḥadīth. For example, they differed on the meaning of certain technical terms in some ḥadīth—terms such as: *al muzābanah,*[9]

9. *Al Muzābanah*—sale of expected yield of a crop for actual produce, for example, the sale of dates on a tree in return for picked dates or of grapes in return for raisins.

al mukhābarah,[10] *al muḥāqalah,*[11] *al mulāmasah,*[12] *al munābadhah,*[13] and *al gharar.*[14]

Occasionally, there might be textual variations in versions of the same ḥadīth to the extent that a key word might be missing from one text, or the entire meaning of the ḥadīth might change because of this missing word. Furthermore, some scholars might receive a ḥadīth which had a consistent internal meaning whereby it was possible to get a good understanding of its intended sense. Others were not so fortunate and their understanding of the ḥadīth would be at variance with the intended sense.

Differences of opinion would also occur when one narrator heard only part of a ḥadīth while another heard it in its entirety. The original text of a ḥadīth might also be changed through misspelling, misrepresentation, or interpolation during the course of transcription—thus resulting in divergent conclusions and judgments. A jurist might also consider a ḥadīth to be sound but at variance with another which he regards as more reliable. He would naturally go by the latter. In another situation, it might not be clear to him which of two pieces of evidence is more reliable and he would refrain from using either until such time as he attains independent confirmation.

A certain jurist might come across information which abrogates a ḥadīth or makes it more specific or limited in scope. Another would not have the benefit of such information and this would of course result in differences in their schools of thought.[15]

Differences over Juristic Methods

This is the third major factor in explaining the emergence of differences of opinion.

---

10. *Al Mukhābarah*—similar to share-cropping, where the right is given by the owner of a plot of land to a farmer to till it in return for some of the produce.

11. *Al Muḥāqalah*—the sale of a crop before it is harvested, as is the current practice in 'futures' markets.

12. *Al Mulāmasah*—a form of sale in pre-Qur'ānic times which is concluded by a buyer touching the goods which at once become his property whether the vendor agreed or not.

13. *Al Munābadhah*—a sale in which a seller would throw an article towards the intending buyer to signify the completion of a sale.

14. *Al Gharar*—a sale in which the goods were not in the possession of the vendor at the time of the contract, nor was the quantity known, nor was it certain that the seller would be able to deliver them in order to fulfill the contract.

15. See *Raf' al Malām*, 7.

Uṣūl al fiqh (sources and principles of jurisprudence) may be defined as the science which embodies knowledge of the proofs or evidences (*adillah;* singular: *dalīl*) on which jurisprudence is founded, the methodology of making deductions from this knowledge, and the subject to which the law applies. All the principles and rules formulated by scholars for regulating the process of ijtihād and deriving subsidiary laws of the Sharī'ah form part of the science of *uṣūl al fiqh*. In their various methodologies, jurists specified the basic principles which they used for formulating laws and they gave the proofs (*ḥujjīyah*) for these laws. They elaborated all the steps they took from the beginning to arrive at a legal ruling.

The scholars of various schools of thought differed in the principles and rules they used. Some, for example, admitted the rulings of Companions of the Prophet as a sound basis for making a judgment on the grounds that a Companion of the Prophet, because of his moral probity, would only give a verdict on the basis of proper evidence, or proper understanding of the evidence, or on the basis of having heard a relevant statement directly from the Prophet which they were unaware of. Others did not place such a great reliance on the rulings of the Companions, choosing to go by only what the companions reported directly from the Prophet and not their interpretations, impressions, or actions.

Some scholars adopted the principle of *al maṣāliḥ al mursalah* (public interest) which is neither commanded nor prohibited in any primary source but is based on the conviction that all the laws of the Sharī'ah are intended for realizing the welfare or the good of mankind. Others did not take this principle as a valid source of law, and this led to actual differences in formulating laws.

There are many other principles of this kind on which the scholars were at variance. They differed over the admissibility of using the principles of "blocking the means to wrongdoing" (*sadd al dharā'i'*); "juristic preference (*istiḥsān*); "presumption of continuity" (*istiṣḥāb*); "adopting the more cautious" (*al akhdh bi al aḥwaṭ*); "adopting the more lenient" (*al akhdh bi al akhaff*); "adopting the more severe" (*al akhdh bi al athqal*); "customary law" (*al 'urf*); and "local custom" (*al 'ādah*). They also differed on the implications of primary texts, the methods of arriving at these implications, and what could justifiably be supported from these texts. In this way, there arose many differences in the field of subsidiary laws.

This is a brief outline of the most important causes for juristic differences. Those who are interested in further research or in finding relevant examples to clarify the various points of difference may draw upon available works, both classical and modern, which deal with these issues.[16]

16. See *Nuzhat al Awliyā',* 392; *Dā'irat Ma'ārif al Qarn al 'Ishrīn* (Twentieth Century Encyclopaedia), 4/141.

Chapter Eight

Knowledge and Refinement

Training and Manners of the *A'immah*

Like the Companions of the first generation and their immediate successors—the *Tābi'ūn*—the leading scholars of the second and third centuries had many differences on issues which required ijtihād. Since their differences were not motivated by any form of egoism or desire to create discord, one can venture to say that they were all on the right path. It is perhaps no exaggeration to say also that these scholars were singularly dedicated to the pursuit of truth and to attaining the pleasure of God. They were highly trained and qualified, and this is why their verdicts were accommodated by scholars of all ages. It was common practice among them to endorse the judgments of those who passed sound verdicts irrespective of the schools of law they belonged to and to ask God's forgiveness for those who seemed to have erred. They had a high mutual regard for one another.

When faced with a difficult issue, some jurists would consult the literature of another school without any hesitation or embarrassment, even though they might not agree on the type of evidence used. They of course felt free to consult any substantiated text. Having arrived at their verdicts, they would issue them with such concluding phrases as "this is more cautious," "this is preferable," "this is how it should be," "I dislike this, or "this does not appeal to me." They did not feel impeded by any unwarranted restrictions or any fear of unfounded accusations. They were easy-going and open-minded, and their concern was to facilitate matters for people.

Among the Companions of the Prophet, their Successors, and the leading scholars after them, there were several differences relating, for example, to the preparation for and the performance of ṣalāh. Some recited the *Basmalah* at the beginning of *Sūrat al Fātiḥah* and others did not. Some uttered it aloud and others did not. Some recited the *Qunūt* supplication as part of the *Ṣalāt al Fajr* (Dawn Prayer) while others did not. Some renewed their *wuḍū'* (ablution) after nose-bleeding, vomiting, and cupping while others did not. Some considered that any physical contact with women nullified *wuḍū'* while others did not. Some renewed their *wuḍū'* after eating camel meat or food cooked on a direct fire while others saw no need for that.

These differences never prevented them from performing ṣalāh behind each other. Abū Ḥanīfah and his followers, as well as al Shāfi'ī and other leading scholars, performed ṣalāh behind the *a'immah* of Madinah from the Mālikī school and others as well, although these *a'immah* did not recite the *Basmalah*, whether silently or audibly. It was reported that Abū Yūsuf, a leading scholar of the Ḥanafī school, performed ṣalāh behind al Rashīd. Abū Yūsuf found later that al Rashīd had been cupped. He did not repeat the *ṣalāh*, although he was of the opinion that cupping nullifies ablution.

Aḥmad ibn Ḥanbal believed that nose-bleeding and cupping nullified ablution. He was asked if people could perform ṣalāh behind an imam who did not renew his ablution after bleeding. He replied: "How could I not pray behind Mālik and Sa'īd ibn al Musayyib?"

According to al Shāfi'ī, the *qunūt* supplication is a firm practice of the Prophet. Yet he is reported to have performed *Ṣalāt al Fajr* near the grave of Abū Ḥanīfah but did not make the *qunūt* supplication. When asked about this, al Shāfi'ī replied: "How can I deviate from him while I am in his presence?" He is also reported to have said: "Perhaps, we have inclined to the school of thought (*madhhab*) of the people of Iraq."[1]

Mālik was the most knowledgeable scholar of ḥadīth transmitted by the people of Madinah and the most accurate in dealing with chains of transmitters (*isnād*). He was also the one most acquainted with the practices of 'Umar ibn al Khaṭṭāb and the sayings of 'Abd Allah ibn 'Umar, 'Ā'ishah, and the seven prominent jurists among the Companions of the Prophet. He was one of the pioneers in establishing the science of ḥadīth reporting and making juristic verdicts. The ḥadīth which he collected and the verdicts he made are contained in his book *Al Muwaṭṭā'*, in which he compiled the reliable *aḥādīth* known to the people of the Hijaz, the sayings of the Companions, and the verdicts of the second generation of Muslims which he verified. The chapters of the book are

1. *Ḥujjat Allāh al Bālighah*, 335.

classified in accordance with the branches of jurisprudence with considerable scholarship.

Al Muwaṭṭā' is the fruit of forty years of scholarly effort. It was the first book on ḥadīth and jurisprudence which appeared in the history of Islam. Its contents were validated by seventy contemporary scholars from the Hijaz. Nonetheless, when the *khalīfah* al Manṣūr wanted to have several copies made and distributed to the new Muslim regions with the intention of getting people to follow its line and thus put an end to differences and dissension, Mālik was the first to reject this suggestion. He is reported to have said to al Manṣūr:

> "Don't do this. People [in various parts of the Muslim lands] already possess a body of knowledge based on reports they have received and sayings of the Prophet they have heard prior to this. Each group of people acts according to what came to it first, and so there are variations in people's practices. Leave the people of each region to follow what they themselves choose."
>
> The *khalīfah* acquiesced in Mālik's wish and prayed that God should grant him success.[2]

Mālik's advice to the *khalīfah* and his refusal to have *al Muwaṭṭā'*– a book he had worked on so scrupulously and for so long – officially prescribed as the standard text of ḥadīth and jurisprudence leave us in no doubt about his breadth of understanding and open-mindedness as well as his complete lack of egoism. He was able to see the limits and dangers of authoritarian rule.

Al Layth's Letter to Mālik

Perhaps one of the best practical examples of the ethics and norms of disagreement was the letter sent to Mālik by al Layth ibn Sa'd, the leading scholar and jurist in Egypt at the time. The letter, in which al Layth gave his views on the various issues on which he differed with Mālik, was a hallmark of knowledge and gracefulness. The letter is too long to quote in full, but here are a few excerpts to illustrate its content and tone:

---

2. Ibid., 307; *al Fikr al Sāmī*, 1/336.

From your letter which I have received, I am pleased to know that you are in good health. May God make your health last and enable you to show gratitude to Him. May He shower more of His abundant goodness on you . . .

You have been informed that I make juristic rulings for people which are at variance with the practice of the people of Madinah. You pointed out that I should fear for my own soul about the verdicts I make for the people here and also that they should follow the practice of the people of Madinah, to which the Prophet migrated and in which the Qur'an was revealed. What you have written in this respect, God willing, is right and I trust that may response to your comments will please you.

Among those who are blessed with knowledge, there is no one who dislikes odd or contrary verdicts more than I, or who has a greater preference for the past scholars of Madinah, or who adopts more readily the verdicts on which they are unanimous. Praise and gratitude are due to God, the Lord and Sustainer of the worlds. No associate has He.

Al Layth ibn Sa'd goes on to state the differences of opinion between him and Mālik over the authority of the practice of the people of Madinah. He points out that many of the early Companions of the Prophet who were brought up under his guidance and instruction had disseminated the teachings of the Qur'an and the Sunnah through various lands as far as they could. He also pointed out that the followers of the second generation had their differences of opinion about many issues. By way of example, he mentions Rabī'ah ibn Abī 'Abd al Raḥmān, but states his disagreement with him on certain matters. Then he says:

In spite of this, praise be to God, Rabī'ah was a person who possessed abundant goodness. He had an original mind and an eloquent tongue. He was a man of obvious grace and good manners, and had a genuine love for his fellow Muslims in general and for us in particular. May God grant him His mercy and forgiveness and the best recompense for his deeds.

Next, Ibn Sa'd mentions some of the issues over which he and Mālik were at variance, for example: combining *Ṣalāt al Maghrib* and *al 'Ishā'* on a rainy night; passing judgment on the evidence of a single witness; paying the delayed portion of a dowry only in the event of a divorce; performing the Prayer for Rain (*Ṣalāt al Istisqā'*) before delivering the *khuṭbah* (sermon).

Ibn Sa'd concludes his letter by saying:

> I have omitted many issues apart from these. I pray that God grants you success and long life because of what I hope people will benefit thereby and because of what I fear they will lose with the passing away of one such as you. Let me assure you of my feeling of nearness to you in spite of the distance that separates us. This is the position of esteem in which I hold you. Do not stop writing to me with news of yourself, your children and family, or if there is anything you want me to do for you personally or for anyone for whom you have a special concern. I would be most pleased to do any service in this regard. At the time of writing this letter, we are in good health, praise be to God. We ask God to enable us to thank Him for what He has favored us with and to continue to bestow His favors on us. May the peace and mercy of God be on you.[3]

There are many discussions and debates recorded in biographical works and historical writings which display great erudition and precision and which are filled with glowing examples of the proper ethics and norms of disagreement. This spirit of enlightened discourse suffered only with the emergence and spread of rigid imitation (taqlīd). This meant that people followed the rulings and practices of a particular school of thought to the exclusion of all others, and even regarded others as deficient or misguided. The result was a hardening of attitudes and positions among scholars and a certain rigidity towards knowledge itself. This was especially true after the passing away of reputable scholars, of whom al Ghazzālī has said:

> Some of the remaining scholars of the second generation continued to uphold the exemplary pattern set up by their predecessors. They adhered steadfastly to the purity of Islam

3. The full text of al Layth's letter is given in *I'lām al Muwaqqi'īn*, 3/83-88; and in *al Fikr al Sāmī*, 1/370-6.

> and the established practice of the early righteous scholars. They shunned close contact with those in political authority and refused to be compromised.

The *khulafā'* out of necessity insisted on appointing them as judges and governors, but when they failed to enlist their approval there were worldly, self-seeking opportunists ready to take the place of the pious and the righteous. In this respect, al Ghazzālī says:

> People of this ilk saw the dignified and honored status of the scholars and the fact that, despite their reluctance and refusal, they were offered positions as *a'immah* and governors. These self-seeking people proceeded to acquire knowledge to fulfill their desire for scholarly repute and positions of honor. They engaged in the study of jurisprudence. They presented themselves to governors and sought their friendship and patronage. Some of them were successful, but none could claim to be free from the degradation and humiliation of pleading for material favors and official ranks. Jurists who were once sought by persons in authority thus became the seekers of patronage and status. They had maintained their integrity and honor through their refusal to bow to persons in authority. Now they were compromised and humiliated by ingratiating themselves with rulers. This is apart from those scholars of God's religion whom the Almighty has blessed with success in every age.[4]

Al Ghazzālī has thus depicted the actual situation of scholars who had become infatuated with the quest for the material world and for whom religion was the only way to reach the gates of princely patronage. In this desire to attain the love of rulers, knowledge was devalued.

Mālik used to say:

> Do not acquire this knowledge [of religion] from four types of people: the foolish and the incompetent; the self-seeking opportunists who seek to propagate their own innovations; the liars who falsify people's reports even if they do not do so using the sayings of the Prophet; and those who are known

4. *Iḥyā' 'Ulūm al Dīn*, 1/14 ff.

> for their goodness, righteousness, and regular performance of worship but who are ignorant of the basis of what they practice and speak about.[5]
>
> He also said:
>
> This knowledge is religion itself. Be careful from whom you acquire your religion. I know of seventy people who, while pointing to the Prophet's mosque, would say: 'The Messenger of God, may God bless him and grant him peace, said while at these very columns . . . ,' but I have never believed anything they said. They were people who would prove to be honest if they were to be entrusted with the public treasury, but when it comes to academic honesty they would fail to live up to that expectation. Thus we avoided consulting these people until Ibn Shihāb came to us and we started to crowd at his door seeking reliable knowledge.[6]

It was unlikely that great disagreements would have occurred amongst people who had these merits and characteristics as those of Ibn Shihāb. Even if difference did occur, they only resulted from the individual's pursuit of the truth for the truth's sake, and not from any egoistical ends. In order to appreciate the standard of ethics and the norms of behavior which the early righteous scholars practiced in dealing with differences, let us look at a few examples of exemplary conduct which they set.

Abū Ḥanīfah and Mālik

We have already alluded to the major difference between the leading scholars, Abū Ḥanīfah and Mālik, and their basic variations in approach when tackling new issues. There was also a marked difference in age between the two men, but all this did not tarnish their mutual respect and fellowship. The famous Qāḍī 'Iyāḍ, in his book *Al Madārik*, recorded that al Layth ibn Sa'd met Mālik in Madinah as he was coming out of a meeting with Abū Ḥanīfah:

---

5. *Al Intiqā'*, 16.
6. Ibid.

"I see that your forehead is bathed in perspiration," said al Layth.

"I sweated in my meeting with Abū Ḥanīfah. He is really a jurist (*faqīh*), O Egyptian!" said Mālik.

Later, al Layth met Abū Ḥanīfah and said to him:

"How excellent are the remarks of this man (Mālik) concerning you!"

"I have not met anyone more quick-witted and truly perceptive than he," acknowledged Abū Ḥanīfah in return.[7]

Muḥammad ibn al Ḥasan and Mālik

Muḥammad ibn al Ḥasan was a very close and prominent colleague of Abū Ḥanīfah and was the one who kept record of his judgments. He left his home and went to live for three years with Imam Mālik, during which he studied *al Muwaṭṭa'* directly from him. One day the two distinguished scholars Muḥammad ibn al Ḥasan and al Shāfi'ī were conferring. Muḥammad ibn al Ḥasan ventured to say:

"Our colleague [meaning Abū Ḥanīfah] is more knowledgeable than yours [meaning Mālik]. Moreover," he added as if to provoke al Shāfi'ī, "it is not befitting that Abū Ḥanīfah should remain silent while Mālik speaks."

Imam al Shāfi'ī replied: "Tell me in all honesty, who is more knowledgeable about the Sunnah of the Prophet, peace be on him—Mālik or Abū Ḥanīfah?"

"Mālik," replied Muḥammad ibn al Ḥasan, and went on to add, "But our colleague [Abū Ḥanīfah] is more informed and skilled in analogy."

Al Shāfi'ī conceded that this was so and went on: "Mālik is more knowledgeable in the Book of God than Abū Ḥanīfah. So whoever is more knowledgeable in the Book of God and in the Sunnah of His Messenger has priority to speak." Muḥammad ibn al Ḥasan could not say anything more.[8]

7. Ibid.
8. Ibid.

Al Shāfi'ī and Muḥammad ibn al Ḥasan

Al Shāfi'ī said: "One day I was having a discussion with Muḥammad ibn al Ḥasan. There was so much talk and disagreement between us that I noticed Ibn al Ḥasan's jugular vein swelling up due to rage and fury."[9] Nonetheless, Muḥammad ibn al Ḥasan said: "If there is any person who disagrees with us and yet is able to convince us of his position, it is al Shāfi'ī." When he was asked why this was so, he replied: "Because of his clarity of mind and exposition, and his certainty in knowledge which shows itself quite clearly in the process of questioning, answering, and listening."[10]

These are some examples of the ethics and norms of proper behavior in disagreement as demonstrated by the leading scholars. From these examples, we can see that the successors of the second generation followed the exemplary patterns set by their righteous forbears. They all drank deeply from the source of prophetic guidance and example. The good conduct of our righteous forbears was not only confined to avoiding defamation and slander, for their overriding concern was for precision and certitude in all their intellectual pursuits. They therefore also steered away from matters about which they had no knowledge and were extremely careful in making juristic rulings lest they should err. Such features of their conduct are evident in a statement made by 'Abd al Raḥmān ibn Abī Laylā, who said:

> In this mosque [the Prophet's mosque in Madinah], I knew one hundred and twenty of the Companions of the Prophet. There is not anyone among them who, if asked about a saying of the Prophet or to give a ruling on an issue, would not wish that some other Companion would reply instead.

In another version he is reported to have said:

> People would present an issue to one of the Companions. This Companion would refrain from passing judgment and would refer the questioner to another Companion. The process would go on until the issue would be referred back to the Companion who had been consulted first.[11]

9. Ibid.
10. *Al Intiqā'*, 38.
11. *Itḥāf al Sādah al Muttaqīn*, 1/278-80.

Muslim scholars in these early times had raised themselves above emotional impulses when issues of knowledge were concerned and were willing to admit any deficiency on their part and defer to others. They would be very circumspect when faced with a critical issue lest they give an erroneous and potentially harmful judgment. A case in point is that of a man who was sent by his people to ask Mālik about a particular issue. It took the man six months to reach Mālik. When the issue was put to Mālik, he said to the man:

> "Tell those who sent you that I have no knowledge about this matter."
>
> "Who then knows about it?" asked the man.
>
> "The one whom Allah has endowed with knowledge," said Mālik and quoted the verse of the Qur'an in which the angels, when asked by God to tell Ādam about the nature of all things, said: "Glory be to You. Of knowledge we have none except what You have taught us" (2: 32).

It is related that on another occasion Mālik was asked about forty-eight issues. To thirty-two of these, his reply was: "I do not know." Also, Khālid ibn Khaddāsh reported: "I came to Mālik from Iraq to ask his opinion on forty issues, and he only answered five of these." Ibn 'Ajlān used to say: "If a learned man failed to understand the wisdom of the saying 'I do not know,' his judgment would be erroneous."

Mālik himself used to quote the saying: "A learned man should instill into his students the habit of saying 'I do not know' so that this habit should become a principle to which they should resort. In this vein, if someone is asked about something he does not know, he should say: 'I do not know.'"

And Abū al Ḍardā', the Companion of the Prophet, is reliably reported as having said: "[To say] 'I do not know' is half of knowledge."

Mālik and Ibn 'Uyaynah

Sufyān Ibn 'Uyaynah[12] was a close associate of Imam Mālik. al Shāfi'ī said that "Were it not for both of them, knowledge in the Hijaz would

12. Sufyān ibn 'Uyaynah (d. 198 AH) was an authority on ḥadīth and a jurist. He was born in Kufah and died in Makkah.

have disappeared."[13] Ibn 'Uyaynah, however, was inclined to defer to Mālik. It is related that once he mentioned a ḥadīth and was afterwards told that Mālik differed with him on the ḥadīth. "Do you compare me with Mālik?" retorted Ibn 'Uyaynah. "My status compared to Mālik's is, as the poet Jarīr says, like the strength of a suckling camel when compared to that of a grown-up one."

Ibn 'Uyaynah related a ḥadīth of the Prophet, peace be on him: "People might travel to the farthest corners of the earth in search of knowledge, but they will not find anyone more knowledgeable than the learned man of Madinah." When asked who was alluded to in this ḥadīth, Ibn Sufyān said it was Mālik ibn Anas and added:

> He [Mālik] never reported any unreliable ḥadīth; he never accepted any ḥadīth from anyone whose trustworthiness and reliability were not beyond question. I have a feeling that Madinah will come to ruin after the death of Mālik ibn Anas.[14]

Mālik and al Shāfi'ī

Al Shāfi'i said:

> Mālik ibn Anas is my teacher. I derive knowledge from him. When people mention scholars, Mālik stands out as a star. There is no one that I trust more wholeheartedly than Mālik ibn Anas."[15]

He also used to say:

> If a ḥadīth is reported by Mālik, its reliability should be readily accepted because if he had any doubt about any ḥadīth he would disregard it completely.[16]

Aḥmad ibn Ḥanbal and Mālik

Abū Zar'a al Dimashqī said:

---

13. *Al Intiqā',* 22.
14. Ibid., 36.
15. Ibid., 23.
16. Ibid., 30.

I heard someone asking Aḥmad ibn Ḥanbal about his stand when faced with a ḥadīth over whose transmission Sufyān and Mālik disagreed. Ibn Ḥanbal replied: "Mālik is dearer to me." "He was then asked, 'What if al Awzā'ī and Mālik were in disagreement?" Ibn Hanbal replied, 'Mālik is preferable in my opinion', although [I regard] al Awzā'ī as one of the leading scholars." Ibn Ḥanbal was then asked about Ibrahim al Nakha'ī without comparing him with Mālik, since al Nakhā'ī was not one of the experts on ḥadīth (*ahl al ḥadīth)*. Ibn Ḥanbal replied: Al Nakha'ī has to be placed among his contemporaries." Then he was asked for his advice about a man who wanted to learn by heart a ḥadīth transmitted by a single individual. He replied: "Let him learn the ḥadīth reported by Mālik."

Opinions on Abū Ḥanīfah

Shu'bah ibn al Ḥajjāj[17] was a leading authority on ḥadīth while Abū Ḥanīfah, as we have already seen, belonged to the school of reasoning (*ahl al ra'ī*). Despite the differences in their methodologies, Shu'bah had a high regard for Abū Ḥanīfah. There was a bond of genuine affection between them and they corresponded with each other. Shu'bah used to authenticate Abū Ḥanīfah's works and request him to speak. When the news of Abū Ḥanīfah's death reached him, he said: "Gone with him is the jurisprudence of Kufah. May God bestow His mercy on him and on us."[18]

When someone asked Yaḥyā ibn Sa'īd al Qaṭṭān about Abū Ḥanīfah, he said: "Conscious of God, he only recommends and extols that knowledge with which God Almighty has endowed him. As for myself, by God whenever I deem any of his pronouncements to be preferable, I adopt them."

This shows that divergence in views did not prevent these scholars from accepting what they perceived to be good from one another. In addition, each would mention the virtues and merits of the other and acknowledge their ideas when they quoted them in support of their own arguments.

---

17. Shu'bah ibn al Ḥajjāj (d. 160 AH) was known as the *Amīr al Mu'minīn* in ḥadīth.
18. *Al Intiqā',* 126.

There are many accounts which tell of the high esteem in which ʻAbd Allāh ibn al Mubārak held Abū Ḥanīfah. He always spoke of him in a favorable manner and attested to his integrity. He often quoted him and praised him. He would not allow anyone to disparage him in his own mosque. One day someone in his circle of students tried to sneer at Abū Ḥanīfah. Ibn al Mubārak said to him: "Be quiet! By God, if you had met Abū Ḥanīfah you would have seen the strength of his intellect and his nobility."

Al Shāfiʻī is reported to have said that he heard Mālik being asked about ʻUthmān al Batti. Mālik replied: "He was a man of average ability." Then he was asked about Ibn Abī Shabramah, and he again said: "He was a man of average ability." Then he was asked about Abū Ḥanīfah, and he replied: "If he came to the brick walls of this mosque and argued with you, saying that they were made of wood, you would really believe that they were wood."[19] This was a pointer to Abū Ḥanīfah's skill in analogical deduction. Al Shāfiʻī's most frequently quoted comment on Abū Ḥanīfah was: "Regarding jurisprudence, people are like dependent children before Abū Ḥanīfah."[20]

In the study sessions and seminars conducted by these scholars, only the good and the beneficial were mentioned. If anyone tried to disregard or contravene the conventions of proper ethics and behavior in which they were conducted, that person would be immediately corrected. He would not be given any chance to slander or sneer at anyone. Al Faḍl ibn Mūsā al Sinanī[21] was asked to comment on those who scornfully attacked Abū Ḥanīfah. He said:

> Abū Ḥanīfah confronted such people with knowledge they could grasp and also with knowledge that they were intellectually not able to grasp. He left them nothing that they could stand on, and they resented him for this.[22]

These are some of the reports and comments which have been made by leading scholars of ḥadīth who used to differ with most of Abū Ḥanīfah's interpretations and conclusions. However, their differences with

---

19. Ibid., 147.

20. Ibid., 136.

21. Al Faḍl ibn Mūsā (d. 191 AH) was from the town of Sīnān in Khurāsān. He was a reliable scholar and an authority on the pronouncements of the second generation of Muslims—the *Tābiʻūn*.

22. *Al Intiqā'.*

him did not prevent them from extolling his virtues and merits, for they were confident that these differences were not motivated by any egoism or arrogance on his part but by the mutual pursuit of truth. Were it not for these high ethical standards and refined manners, a great deal of the jurisprudence of our early and respected scholars would have fallen into oblivion or been cast aside. These scholars came to the defense of other scholars only because they knew that their responsibility was to safeguard Islamic jurisprudence, which is indispensable for the moral protection and well-being of the Muslim Ummah.

Opinions on al Shāfiʻī

Ibn ʻUyaynah was a distinguished scholar and one who was held in high esteem. Yet when people came to him for an explanation of some point in the Qur'an or for a judicial ruling, he would refer them to al Shāfiʻī with the words: "Ask this person." Often, on seeing al Shāfiʻī he would say: "This is the best young man of his time." And when he heard of the death of al Shāfiʻī, he said: "If Muḥammad ibn Idrīs has died, then the best man of his time has died."

Yaḥyā ibn Saʻīd al Qaṭṭān used to say: "I pray to God for al Shāfiʻī even in my ṣalāh." ʻAbd Allāh ibn ʻAbd al Ḥakam and his son Muḥammad were followers of the Mālikī school of thought, but the father advised the son to remain close to al Shāfiʻī because he had not seen anyone who had "more insight into the principles of knowledge or jurisprudence." It seems that Muḥammad acted on his father's advice because he is reported to have said: "Had it not been for al Shāfiʻī, I would not have known how to reply to anyone's argument. Through him I have learnt whatever I have. He is the one, may God bless him, who instructed me in analogical reasoning and he was an upholder of the Sunnah and established practice. He was a good and virtuous person. He had an eloquent tongue and a firm, exacting intellect."[23]

Aḥmad and al Shāfiʻī

ʻAbd Allāh, the son of Imam Aḥmad ibn Ḥanbal, once asked his father:

23. Ibid., 73.

"What sort of person was al Shāfi'ī? I hear you frequently praying for him."

"Al Shāfi'ī, may God bless him," said his father, "was like the sun to the world, and like good health to people. Can you think of any substitute or compensation for these two vital necessities?"

Ṣāliḥ, another son of Aḥmad ibn Ḥanbal, was met by Yaḥyā ibn Mu'īn who asked him:

"Isn't your father ashamed of what he is doing?"

"What is he doing?" asked Ṣāliḥ.

"I saw him with al Shāfi'ī," said Yaḥyā. "Al Shāf'ī was riding and he was on foot holding the rein of al Shāfi'ī's mount."

Ṣāliḥ later related this to his father who said:

"If you see him again, tell him that I say that if he wishes to gain true knowledge and understanding, let him come and take hold of the other side of the reins of al Shāfi'ī's mount."[24]

Abū Ḥumayd ibn Aḥmad al Baṣrī reported that he was one day discussing a certain issue with Aḥmad ibn Ḥanbal. A man from the audience told Ibn Ḥanbal that there was no authentic ḥadīth on that issue. "If there is no authentic ḥadīth on this issue, there is al Shāfi'ī's pronouncement on it, and the proofs he has used are the most reliable on this issue," replied Ibn Ḥanbal, thus demonstrating his confidence in al Shāfi'ī's scholarship. He later asked al Shāfi'ī for his ruling on a certain matter which the latter gave. Aḥmad then asked him: "On what basis have you pronounced this ruling? Is there a ḥadīth or written document on it?" Al Shāfi'ī replied that there was and he produced a relevant authentic ḥadīth of the Prophet, peace be on him.[25] Aḥmad ibn Ḥanbal is also reported to have said: "If I were asked a question on which I do not know a relevant saying (*khabar*), I would say: 'Al Shāfi'ī says . . . ,' because he is an imam and a scholar from the Quraysh."[26]

---

24. Ibid.
25. *Ādāb al Shāfi'ī wa Manāqibuhu* (The Manners and Traits of al Shāfi'ī), 86-7.
26. Ibid., 86.

Dāwūd ibn 'Alī al Iṣbahānī reported that he heard Isḥāq ibn Rāhawayh say: "Aḥmad ibn Ḥanbal met me in Makkah and said to me: 'Come with me and let me introduce you to a man the like of whom you have never seen,' and he showed me al Shāfi'ī." Such was the high esteem in which Aḥmad ibn Ḥanbal held al Shāfi'ī. It is not strange for a student to be fond of and grateful to his teacher. But al Shāfi'ī himself in return acknowledged his student's excellence and his knowledge of the Sunnah by saying to him: "You are more knowledgeable in ḥadīth and in the biography of ḥadīth narrators than I. If you hear of any authentic hadīth, let me know whether it is related in Kufah, Basrah, or Syria. I will refer to it if it proves to be authentic."[27]

Al Shāfi'ī had such a high regard for Ibn Ḥanbal that he would not mention his name but would refer to him as "the reliable and trustworthy one" among his colleagues.[28]

These are just glimpses[29] which clearly show the high standards of ethics and behavior practiced by the eminent scholars of early times. These high standards were not affected by differences in approach and methodologies. These righteous forbears of ours were brought up into and guided by the teachings and exemplary patterns set by the noble Prophet, peace be on him. Selfish motives and impulses did not get the better of them in their rigorous pursuit of knowledge. Biographies and history books are replete with instances of scholarly interaction conducted in an intellectually exacting but highly refined and gracious manner according to the best traditions of Islam. This is an object lesson for us today, fragmented and disparate as we are. We need to return to this level of consciousness and refined and gracious behavior which our noble ancestors have demonstrated. This must be done if we are indeed serious in striving to reconstruct a truly Islamic pattern of life.

Admittedly, there were instances in which these lofty Islamic standards were not observed. But the responsibility for this failure lies with unthinking followers or recalcitrant individuals who became steeped in bigotry and fanaticism. These individuals or groups failed to perceive the true "scientific" spirit in scholarly interaction which accounted for the differences among jurists. Nor did they have any insight into the

---

27. *Al Intiqā'*, 75.

28. Ibn al Jawzī, *Manāqib al Imām Aḥmad* (The Traits of Imām Aḥmad), 116.

29. There is an urgent need to gather the legacy of the Ummah in this field and present it in an accessible and attractive form. We pray that the opportunity and the means for doing so will be made available.

sublime norms of proper *ādāb* which emanate from pure intentions, a genuine search for truth, and a desire to ascertain the purpose of the Lawgiver. They were, it seems, the type of people about whom al Ghazzālī said:

> The jurists have become seekers [of favor and status] after they were once sought [for their knowledge and integrity]. They were highly respected when they shunned the blandishments of those in political authority, but they have now become disgraced by succumbing to them.

The one who is sought for his knowledge and integrity is the one who is free and is a master of himself; he does not deviate from the truth. The one who is a seeker of favor and status sells himself and is only concerned with pleasing his master.

Unthinking followers and self-seeking individuals set differences of opinion into a totally negative mold. Differences of opinion among genuine scholars were, to begin with, a source of blessing which helped develop Islamic jurisprudence, establish the relevance of Islam to changing circumstances, and safeguard public welfare. Later, differences of opinion became one of the most critical and dangerous factors contributing to disunity and internecine strife among Muslims. Indeed it became a scourge which dissipated much of the energies and potential of the Muslim Ummah; it caused people to become engrossed in matters which did not deserve the attention given to them.

Chapter Nine

After the Illustrious Age

Analytical thought (ijtihād) in jurisprudence came to an end in the fourth century of the Muslim era, while blind imitation (*taqlīd*) began to flourish.

The first and second centuries did not witness any such practice as passing judgments either on the basis of unsubstantiated utterances or on the accounts and conclusions of one scholar to the exclusion of others. During the third century, analytical thought was still very vigorous. Some scholars might have relied upon the rules, principles, and methods of deduction handed down by their predecessors, but they never clung blindly to their pronouncements and conclusions.

People in the fourth century may be divided into scholars on the one hand and the general public on the other. The general public depended on the scholars for transmitting to them the body of agreed-upon knowledge from the original sources on which there was unanimity among the scholars. This included knowledge of such matters as purification (*ṭahārah*), the performance of ṣalāh, ṣawm, and the collection and distribution of zakāh. If they were faced with any problematic details, people would seek help from any scholar regardless of the school of thought to which he belonged.

As for the specialist scholars, they were engaged in the study of ḥadīth and the legal legacy of the Companions of the Prophet and the generation that followed them. If they were faced with an issue on which they did not find any satisfactory or clear-cut answer in the original sources, they would turn to the pronouncements of previous jurists, choosing whichever verdict seemed more sound and reliable, whether it originated in the school of Madinah or of Kufah.

The scholars engaged in this task of interpretation would thoroughly research the different schools of thought. If a scholar arrived at a judgment based on a particular school he would, for example, be described as a Shāfi'ī or a Ḥanafī without his having in fact any firm or sole attachment to that particular school, as later happened. Some of the scholars of ḥadīth in fact identified with particular schools of thought to promote mutual agreement. Al Nasā'ī, al Bayhaqī, and al Khiṭābī identified with the Shāfi'ī school, for example. However, only a *mujtahid* or one who was capable of analytical thought and making independent judgments could hold the position of a judge, and no *'ālim* was called a *faqīh* unless he was a *mujtahid.*

Split between Political and Intellectual Leadership

The situation changed noticeably after the fourth *hijrī* century. Al Ghazzālī (d. 505 AH) described the situation thus:

> Know that after the Messenger of God, may God's peace and blessings be on him, the *khilāfah* was held by the rightly-guided *khulafā'.* They were leaders and scholars who were conscious of God Almighty. They were jurists who had a deep understanding of God's laws and were actively engaged in tackling problems and passing legal judgments. [So competent were they that] they rarely sought the help of jurists in dealing with actual situations, and when they did it was for the sake of consultation. Thereafter the *khilāfah* passed to people who did not deserve to be rulers and who lacked the competence even to formulate their own decisions. They were forced to seek the help of jurists. They cultivated the friendship of scholars in order to get assistance in making legislation of all kinds. There still existed some scholars of the same mettle as those of earlier generations. They maintained a clear vision of the requirements of the religion, and when they were approached by ambitious rulers with various blandishments to accept positions as judges and administrators they did not compromise their integrity.
>
> People in these times saw the great esteem in which scholars were held and the attempt by leaders and rulers to attract them. The desire to gain esteem with the public and favors from rulers encouraged people to enter the field of education and to apply themselves eagerly to making legal judgments. They ingratiated themselves with the rulers, sought entry into their

political circles, and tried to gain positions of authority. Some succeeded and others did not. Those who succeeded were not free from the taint of subservience and degradation. This was the process by which jurists, who were once highly honored and sought after, became devalued seekers of patronage from rulers.

In this age, however, there were some who, through the grace of God, remained genuine scholars of God's religion. But most of those who turned to dealing with legal problems and passing verdicts did so because of the pressing need for such persons in the new districts and governorates.

In the wake of these new types of jurists came ministers and princes who listened indiscriminately to whatever people said with regard to the basic principles of faith . . . People turned eagerly to argumentation and scholastic theology (*kalām*). An abundance of literary works appeared on the subject. People classified the various processes of argumentation and developed the art of discovering contradictions and discrepancies in the pronouncements of others. They claimed that their expositions were for the defense of God's religion, guarding the Sunnah, and curbing malicious innovators. The same claim of protecting religion was made by those who busied themselves in passing legal judgments (*fatāwā*). They claimed that they were protecting the religion and that they assumed control of the laws of Muslims out of concern for God's creatures and out of the desire to offer sincere advice to them.

Thereafter, there appeared those who did not approve of the damage caused by scholastic theology and the subsequent opening of the floodgate of disputation which gave rise to terrible fanaticisms and animosities which, in turn, led to bloodshed and the destruction of Muslim lands. Such persons began to look back to the jurisprudence of earlier times, and in particular to the schools of thought of al Shāfi'ī and Abū Ḥanīfah, may God be pleased with them both. People abandoned scholastic theology and the subtleties of disputation. They turned instead to the controversial questions posed by al Shāfi'ī and Abū Ḥanīfah in particular, while tending to disregard those posed by Mālik, Sufyān,[1] and Aḥmad ibn Ḥanbal, may God Almighty bless them and others like them. They claimed that their objective was to deduce the finer points of the Sharī'ah, to establish the *raison d'être* of each school of thought, and to systematize the principles on which legal judgments should be based. Consequently, they came up with many classifications and methods of deduction on the basis of which they categorized the types of dialectical debates.

They have continued in this manner up till now. We do not know what God has in store for the times after us. This, then, is the impetus which drives people on to disputation and competitive debates. There is no other cause. If these opportunistic and overweening scholars had inclined towards disagreement with any of the leading scholars on any aspect of knowledge, they would probably have limped after them also. They would have kept on insisting though that their only concern, in all their endeavors, was to attain to knowledge of the religion itself and to seek nearness to God, the Lord and Sustainer of all the worlds.[2]

In the above analysis, al Ghazzālī put his finger on the real disease which afflicted the Ummah in the era after the rightly-guided, scholarly leaders. This disease emanated essentially from the critical split in the Muslim leadership between the intellectual on the one hand and the political on the other. Our history has since been characterized by this distortion which still plagues us. Political practices contrary to Islamic norms were put in place. This stemmed from the rulers' ignorance of Islamic political theory and practice. On the intellectual front, there is only a theoretical, hypothetical appreciation of an Islamic system which is not rooted in the actual experience and problems of the Muslims. This theoretical approach could not deal with everyday problems in a practical manner as the *Ṣaḥābah* and the *Tābi'ūn* had done. The majority of juridical problems and many of the issues relating to jurisprudence were nothing but theoretical formulations produced in the course of competitive debates and in an atmosphere of dissension.

---

1. According to al Ghazzālī, there were five *mujtahidūn* whose schools of thought were followed. In addition to the four well-known ones, the fifth was Sufyān al Thawrī.
2. *Iḥyā' 'Ulūm al Dīn*, 1/14 ff.

Loopholes and Stratagems

After this disastrous trend, jurisprudence tended to become a means for justifying the existing status quo rather than a means for regulating people's lives and circumstances according to the requirements of the Sharī'ah. This approach to law and legislation gave rise to unusual anguish on the part of Muslims, for they frequently saw that the same act committed by the same person and at the same time and place was regarded by one jurist as lawful and by another as unlawful. This predicament is adequately demonstrated by the fact that there came into existence a principle of jurisprudence which is dealt with in voluminous chapters called "Loopholes and Stratagems" (*Al Makhārij wa al Ḥiyal*).[3] This "principle" is concerned with seeking to evade the admitted purport and consequences of the law through devising loopholes and "legal" stratagems and expedients.

Ingenuity and skill in dealing with this "principle" of jurisprudence came to be regarded as evidence of the intellectual capacity of a jurist and of his genius and excellence over others. As time went by and the authority of religion dwindled, this phenomenon assumed alarming proportions. People became careless about the Sharī'ah, and those who had the responsibility for making legal decisions started to pass verdicts which were not based on any evidence and which they themselves did not regard as sound. They claimed that they passed these verdicts either in order to facilitate matters for people or to be severe on them so as to prevent them from transgressing the limits (*ḥudūd*) of the Sharī'ah. This was particularly true of the dispensations they granted to rulers on the one hand and of the exactions they made on the common people on the other.[4]

Here are a few examples of verdicts passed at that time:

- A jurist, asked about the validity of the *wuḍū'* of someone who touched a woman or who touched his genitals,

3. *Al Makhārij wa al Ḥiyal* (Loopholes and Legal Stratagems) is considered as one of the 'principles' (*aṣl*) of the Ḥanafī school of law. A book on the subject was written by Imam Muḥammad ibn al Ḥasan which was later commented upon at length. There is a doctoral thesis on the subject by Muḥammad Buḥayrī entitled *Al Ḥiyal fī al Sharī'ah al Islamīyah* (Legal Stratagems in Islamic Law).

4. Sallām Madkūr, *Manāhij al Ijtihād fī al Islām* (Methodologies of Independent Reasoning in Islam), 450-1; also Ḥamad al Kubaysī, *Uṣūl al Aḥkām* (The Principles of Laws), 390.

would say: "According to Abū Ḥanīfah, the *wuḍū'* is not nullified."

- If asked about playing chess or eating horsemeat, he would say: "According to al Shāfi'ī, these things are lawful."
- If asked about the punishment of a person who made a false allegation or about exceeding the limits in the case of discretionary punishments set by a judiciary, he would say: "Malik sanctioned that practice."
- If a jurist wanted to use a legal stratagem (*ḥīlah*) to enable someone to sell off an endowment in perpetuity (*waqf*) which had fallen into ruin and was not yielding any benefit, and moreover whose administrator had no means of developing it, the jurist would legislate that selling the *waqf* was permissible according to Ibn Ḥanbal. The consequence of this verdict was that Muslim charitable endowments, which had always been considered inviolable, became private property in a matter of a few years.[5]

By this process and through the loss of *taqwā*, the purposes of the Sharī'ah were subverted and its holistic principles were overlooked. The matter came to such a pass that frivolous and insolent poets such as Abū Nuwās began to ridicule the laws of God with poetry such as this:

The Iraqi has allowed fermented juice and its imbibing;
Forbidden only is wine and drunkenness, he said.
Both drinks are one and the same, said the Ḥijazi.
Free now to choose between both pronouncements.
Khamr is now lawful for us!
I shall press their statements to their utmost limits,
And have my draughts of this wine
To rid myself of life's cares.

The public who was expected to protect the integrity of the religion, became degraded, and religion itself became devalued in the sight of people. Overstepping the limits of the religion became acceptable in the public's, eyes as they sought to make things too easy for themselves.

5. See Shakīb Arslān, *al Irtisāmāt al Liṭāf.*

Some jurists succumbed to this permissive trend and destroyed the protecting walls of reverence and awe for the Sharī'ah. They allowed themselves to pass judgments to suit their whims and impulses.

Sternness and Sterility

At the other extreme, they were confronted by a stern and stubborn group who sought out the strictest and severest opinions on which to base their juristic judgments. This group thought that they were serving Islam through this get-tough policy and that they would persuade people to abide by the requirements of the religion. This was not to be. The result of the hard-line approach was—as it usually is—contrary to what they had expected. People became alienated from Islamic teachings and the Sharī'ah. They refused to comply with it and they saw in it hardship instead of ease.

There is the story of the Andalusian monarch who asked the Mālikī jurist Yaḥyā ibn Yaḥyā[6] what he should do to atone for having intercourse with his wife during the daytime in Ramaḍān. Yaḥyā told him that he had to fast for two consecutive months. When he was asked why he had not given the monarch the first option of setting free someone in bondage, he replied: "He is capable of setting hundreds of slaves free. Therefore, he must have the harder punishment, which is fasting."

Islam is practical. It makes things easy rather than difficult for people. It encourages people to respond willingly and naturally to its laws and seeks to avoid distress and hardship. At the same time, it does not leave people to roam in absolute freedom and succumb to all their passions and impulses. This is the spirit in which judicial rulings should be made. It is clear from this that both the permissive and the excessively harsh tendencies among jurists at that time were not in keeping with the purpose of the wise Lawgiver.

The task of the scholar is to transmit the message of God Almighty to people as it was revealed in the Qur'an and as the Prophet taught it. It is not for him to incline arbitrarily to harshness on the one hand or leniency on the other.

> "Say: Will you instruct God about your religion!" (49: 16)
> "Say: Do you know better than God?" (2: 140)

---

6. Yaḥyā ibn Yaḥyā al Laythī (d.234AH) studied the *Muwaṭṭā'* from Mālik and propagated his school of thought in North Africa and Spain. See *al Bidāyah*, 10/312.

The lesson to be derived from these two Qur'anic verses is that we have a duty to adopt the wisdom and follow the divine teachings of the Qur'an and eschew innovation, whether it stems from a tendency to arbitrary harshness or a tendency to arbitrary leniency.

Taqlīd and Its Aftermath

We have seen above how chaotic and ridiculous the state of juristic reasoning had become. Many righteous and concerned people feared that incompetent and unreliable people would only corrupt the process of ijtihād. Men who were at the bidding of rulers assumed the task of making legal verdicts. Without any scruples, they began to twist the texts (*nuṣūṣ*) of the original sources to suit their own inclinations and purposes. Scholars fluctuated between arbitrary leniency and harshness. Righteous people feared for the very destiny of the Muslim community and for the religion itself. They began searching for a cure and the only solution they could find was to bind the Ummah to taqlīd! What a crisis it was that the only way out should be a retreat into blind imitation!

The jostling and the constant bickering among the jurists, their opposing and mutually exclusive views, and their unending resistance to one another seemed to point to only one way out: a return to the pronouncements of scholars of old on controversial questions. The people themselves, having lost confidence in many of the judges, began to put their trust only in those whose rulings conformed to pronouncements of one of the four *a'immah*—Abū Ḥanīfah, Mālik, al Shāfi'ī, and Ibn Ḥanbal.

Among the Muslim masses, following one of the four *a'immah*, sticking to everything they said, and steering clear from whatever they did not say became the bastion against deviant rulings issued by suspect *mujtahidūn* for their own ends. Imam al Ḥaramayn (d. 478 AH) claimed that there was a consensus (*ijmā'*) among specialist scholars prohibiting the taqlīd of eminent Companions of the Prophet. Instead, according to this alleged consensus, people were required to follow the schools of thought of the four *a'immah* because they had thoroughly examined all the sources and the context of the various legal issues and properly classified them. They had also studied the methods and pronouncements of the early Muslims and so there was no need to go back directly to these sources. Imam al Ḥaramayn supported this alleged consensus and came to the strange judgment that the common Muslim is under obligation to follow the schools of thought of these unquestionably knowledgeable and precise scholars.[7]

On the basis of the pronouncement of Imam al Ḥaramayn and the alleged consensus of specialist scholars, Ibn al Ṣalāḥ issued his claim that it was obligatory to follow the four *a'immah* due to the textual authenticity, the disciplined approach, and the sound methods of reasoning and interpretation which marked their schools of thought. The Companions of the Prophet and their immediate successors, according to him, did not have these advantages.[8]

As a consequence of this total reliance on the four schools of thought, people became negligent and careless about the study of the Qur'an and the sciences associated with it, and they turned away from direct study of the Sunnah and its disciplines. They became content with knowledge that was neatly packaged and handed down, and all they had to do was to establish it firmly, defend it vigorously, and apply it as best as they could.

As this decline continued, the spirit of dissension grew stronger and spread. And for centuries thereafter, blind imitation became the norm. Intellectual thought stagnated. The tree of independent reasoning withered. Ignorance became common. Civil strife reared its ugly head. The *'ālim* and the *faqīh*, in the eyes of people, became the one who had memorized a collection of the pronouncements of earlier jurists and equipped himself with some of their opinions without being able to distinguish between what was weak and what was reliable. The ḥadīth 'scholar' became someone who had memorized a collection of *ahādīth*; whether it was authentic or spurious did not matter.

This deplorable situation did not end there but worsened considerably, as if knowledge had disappeared from the world of Muslims afflicted by intellectual sterility. In this atmosphere, harmful innovation, perversion, and corruption of various kinds flourished. All this left the door wide open for the enemies of Islam to sweep away Islamic civilization and plunder its heartlands.

The Ummah in Recent Times

This was the condition of the Ummah as it slumbered and stagnated due to taqlīd, dreaming of the grandeur of a glorious past. Since the

---

7. *Al Burhān*, 2/1146; *al Taqrīr wa al Taḥbīr*, 3/353.
8. *Al Taqrīr wa al Taḥbīr*, 3/353.

emergence of the split between the executive and the judiciary, the masses of Muslims were caught up in a state of bewilderment and tossed about by their own interests and impulses. The scholars of the Ummah were so busy justifying their own positions that if anyone had studied the legacy of this Ummah, which had dazzled the world with its unprecedented achievements, he would hardly believe that such intellectual rigidity and sterility could stem from the earlier enlightened and vibrant generations.

This was the state of the Ummah as the modern European renaissance got underway. The Europeans saw before them a Muslim Ummah which had lost virtually everything of its real vitality. Nothing of any substance remained. The faith was dormant and the Muslims themselves were bewildered. There was no longer any of the old certainty. Behavior had become deviant. Steadfastness was lacking. Intellectual thought was rigid. Ijtihād was suspended. The science of jurisprudence was lost. Innovations were rampant. The Sunnah was laid to rest and Islamic consciousness grew dim and all but vanished. It was as if the Ummah with all its special characteristics was no longer itself.

These conditions made the Ummah an easy prey for the Western powers who were lying in wait for this golden opportunity to move in and finish off the little that remained of Islamic character. This has led to the situation in which we are today. It is a situation of ignominy and subjugation. We no longer appear to be capable of conducting our own affairs; they are in the hands of our enemies who decide our destiny. Indeed, we beg them to find solutions for problems which are of our own making.

During this period, the Ummah has tried to gather what remained of its strength to win back its lost glory and recover its balance. All attempts in this direction, however, have ended up in failure because the means adopted were flawed and not in accordance with the natural laws and patterns set by God. These attempts have been based on adopting and following alien paradigms and aping the foreign masters, both of which have only compounded the predicament.

Meanwhile, a new generation in search of a healing balm has begun to explore solutions that are sound and authentically Islamic. Various emerging groups of Muslims have begun to realize that "the means for rectifying the condition of the Ummah at this stage in its history must be the same means which were used to set it on the right course at the very beginning." They have thus turned to Islam and realized how sweet and satisfying it is. This has produced the phenomenon called the "Islamic Reawakening."

The enemies of Islam, despite their own internal differences, never wanted to give a free scope to this blessed awakening. How many are the arms and resources which they have used to combat us! Some within the Muslim ranks are also part of this armory and have been used as agents to sabotage the movement for reconstructing the Ummah in the true light of Islam. One of the most devastating methods used by the enemy was the strategy of "divide and rule." This was facilitated by the existence of rampant discord (*ikhtilāf*) in the Muslim Ummah. The Islamic awakening soon found itself facing the grievous challenge of disagreements (*ikhtilāf*) over and above the many other challenges which consumed the energies of the sincere workers for Islam. Energies were further dissipated on the perilous rock of discord. Some among the youth identified themselves with the early righteous forbears (the *salafīyah*) and others with the upholders of ḥadīth (*ahl al ḥadīth*); one group identified itself with a particular school of thought (*madhhab*) while others did not see the necessity for this. Among these groups, various accusations of unbelief, blasphemy, harmful innovation, treachery, spying, and so on are bandied about. All of these accusations ought not to be exchanged between fellow Muslims let alone publicized through all the available media in total disregard of the fact that the malicious attempts to extinguish the light of Islam are more dangerous to the survival of the Ummah than these differences.

In retrospect, we can see that the leading scholars of the schools of Islamic jurisprudence had reasons to justify their differences of opinion and lessen their impact. The master perpetrators of disagreement in our times, however, do not have a single plausible basis for justifying their differences. They are not *mujtahidūn* or persons capable of independent reasoning or analytical thought. They are, rather, unthinking followers (*muqallidūn*) of those among them who raise their voices to proclaim that they are not in fact 'followers' nor do they believe in the 'duty to follow.' They claim that they derive their rulings and opinions directly from the Qur'an and the Sunnah of the Prophet, peace be on him. In reality, they cling to some books of ḥadīth and follow in the footsteps of their authors in all matters pertaining to the authenticity of a ḥadīth and the trustworthiness and reliability of its narrators. Some of them claim knowledge of the science which studies the biographies of ḥadīth reporters and the extent of their reliability. On the basis of studying a single book on this vast subject, a person cannot justifiably elevate himself to the position of a *mujtahid*.

It is only appropriate that someone who has acquired some real knowledge should not behave like an ignorant person and hurl accusations and insults against others. He should realize the grave dangers facing the Islamic faith and seek to ward off these dangers. He should be keenly concerned to bring together the hearts and minds of people even while they follow different schools of thought. At least they should stick scrupulously to the ethics and norms (*adab*) of proper behavior when differences do arise, as did the noble scholars of the past.

Sincere Muslims had hoped that the Islamic awakening would at least achieve two objectives. Firstly, it was hoped that it would put an end to heretical and atheistic ideals, and false and corrupt ideologies and influences. In so doing, it was hoped that it would purify the hearts and minds of many in Muslim society and re-instill in them the true Islamic faith. Secondly, it would then propagate the Islamic message throughout the world and make the word of God supreme on earth.

It is extremely painful to note that some within the Muslim ranks have deliberately sought to clip the wings of this awakening by shackling it with the fetters of discord where this was totally unnecessary. The result is that Muslims are distracted by their own mostly petty quarrels; their efforts are dissipated; issues have become so confused and mixed up that they are unable to distinguish between trivial and important matters. How, one may well ask, can such a people deal with their problems according to the level of their importance and order their priorities in such a way as to bring about an effective renewal of Islamic life?

The effects of discord (*khilāf*) among Muslims or the perpetuation of its causes is, it must be stressed, a great treason to the goals of Islam. It is tantamount to destroying the contemporary Islamic awakening which has revitalized the hopes and aspirations of Muslims. It is a hindrance to the onward march of Islam. It dissipates the sincere efforts of those striving in the cause of Islam and would incur the displeasure of God. Today, for these reasons, one of the most important obligations on Muslims in general and on those who work for Islam in particular – after belief in God Almighty – is to work for the unification of all Islamic groups and elements and to eradicate all factors causing discord among them. If this goal proves impossible to achieve, then let us keep our differences to the minimum and well within the ethics and norms of behavior set by our righteous forbears. Differences of opinion do not prevent a genuine meeting of hearts in order to bring about a renewal of the noble Islamic life. This can be achieved only when intentions are sincere and purely for the sake of God Almighty. When this becomes a reality, support and success from God will not be denied.

Causes of Differences Today

The causes of differences of opinion naturally differ from one age to another. Each age will naturally bequeath some of its problems to a succeeding age. Today, one of the most important and conspicuous causes of differences between Muslims is ignorance of Islam or a deficient knowledge of Islam.

The state of education of Muslims before the arrival of aggressive colonialism was deplorable, and it became increasingly worse after the penetration of colonialism in Muslim lands. The occupiers knew precisely where the Muslim Ummah was most vulnerable, and so began to put in place educational programs and institutions for colonializing Muslim minds and changing their ideas to conform to their own interests and worldview. This policy of infiltration was calculated to make the Muslims accept the new anti-Islamic world order in the name of progress and modernization on the European model. They argued that this rise of progress and civilization in Europe was only possible through the overthrowing of religion-based laws and loosening the stranglehold of the church. Religion as such, they argued, was nothing more than an impediment that prevented humanity from attaining freedom and prosperity.

These claims might very well be true with regard to Christianity and other religions; they certainly cannot be applied to Islam, for Islam promotes human happiness and the realization of human potentialities and is guided by the light of God. In the effort to sever the Muslim Ummah from the mainsprings of its existence and its Islamic moorings, the imperialists placed obstacles and sanctions against Islamic education and the Arabic language which is the medium of Islamic education. To realize this objective, students who sought an Islamic education found themselves neglected and devalued. The studies they pursued were also underrated, and they were denied the professional education and training that would enable them to get decent jobs and salaries. On the other hand, students who enrolled in the modern schools on the colonialist patterns were given special care and attention. The doors of opportunity were opened before them and they were groomed as the new leaders of the Ummah. In this way the grip tightened around the necks of those interested in Islamic education and the Arabic language. The avenues for seeking such an education were blocked.

In most Muslim countries, soon only a few turned to Islamic education and eventually standards dropped. Most of those who wanted such an education became like the one who tills the soil but does not expect to reap any produce. Only specific circumstances encouraged them to seek such an education. They did not have the strength to free themselves from its hold even after graduation, for the way remained blocked before them. They did not have the capacity to perform the role which a scholar should perform in society and bring to fruition the message with which he is entrusted. With the doors of opportunity blocked, they lost their independence, their personalities weakened, and they were induced to join the official religious organizations set up, in advance, to serve preplanned and limited objectives. They were unable to get beyond these inasmuch as they were denied the opportunity to perform their proper role in society. As a result, people lost faith in them.

In the attempt to deepen the gulf between the Ummah and its faith and to cut the roots which connected it with the Sharī'ah, the anti-Islamic imperialists tried to place Islamic education and the teaching of Arabic in the background. The field was left open for alien concepts and ideologies which were attractively presented to the youth but only exposed them to pain, worry, and bitterness. Every type of ideology was presented to them – from communism to socialism, and from radicalism to nationalism and democracy. However beautifully each was packaged, it only served to increase the ignominy and disgrace of the Muslim Ummah to an unprecedented level.

It became clear to many Muslims, however, that Islam alone was capable of curing the problems of the Ummah, uplifting it from its decline, and arresting the causes of decadence. After groping aimlessly in the darkness, they decided on their own to turn to Islam out of concern for themselves and their religion. When they came up against the problem of properly understanding the religion and acquiring a knowledge of its laws, they resorted to books which could not give them a sound, complete, and comprehensive understanding of this system. They were unable to acquire a knowledge of its purposes and of its holistic nature—just like the group of blind men who passed their hands over different parts of an elephant's body, each one insisting that the part he touched was the elephant. This is the condition of Muslims in relation to Islam today.

The Muslim Ummah has been split up into small groups and factions. There are those who have turned their backs on Islam and oscillate between the East and the West as if their only connection with Islam were their names and the past legacy of Islam. Were it not for a certain timidity, they would perhaps sever all connection with Islam. There are others who yearn to come back to Islam, but when they do they go along different paths and end up disagreeing among themselves. This makes them an easy prey for the enemies of Islam. Everywhere, rulers surround them and offer them no way out. They are finished off completely before they are able to recover their balance and find the straight way.

The Way to Recovery

Now that the disease which has plagued the Ummah for so long has been identified, we need to produce a remedy and chart a course towards recovery.

Sincere Muslims engaged in the field of promoting Islam and who are deeply conscious of the painful reality of the Muslim situation should identify groups of talented Muslim youths and make available to them the best means to study the sciences of the Sharī'ah. This should be at the hands of the few remaining scholars who are known for their depth of knowledge, uprightness, piety, and constructive thought and who have a sound insight into the purposes and holistic nature of the Sharī'ah as well as a good understanding of its component sciences. These scholars should adopt the educational principles and methods of the noble Prophet. This body of talented Muslim youths should also be trained by another group who are well equipped with knowledge of the various contemporary sciences and who have a high level of sincerity and piety. This combination will hopefully set the pace for an Islamic awakening and help the Ummah recover its strength and integrity. In the process, it will reassume its leading role and rescue humanity from rushing headlong, day by day, into disaster. There is no salvation for humanity except through Islam.

Secondly, Muslims are living through an intellectual crisis whose dimensions are perceived only by a small minority. In order to tackle this crisis, Muslims must rectify their manner of thinking. The crisis is distinctly manifest in the collapse of the Ummah's institutions; in the non-existence of properly organized bodies; in the low levels of consciousness, knowledge, and training of young Muslims; in the disintegration of mutual bonds between believers; in the corruption and deviation of most of the leaders in the Muslim world; in all the malicious endeavors to sabotage the well-intentioned efforts of groups of upright and pious Muslims. All this is due to the fact that Islam is far away from the lives of Muslims. There is a yawning gap between the ideals of Islam and the realities of the Muslim world. Non-Muslims see Islam as a cloud which produces no rain and therefore does not quicken the dead earth or they see it as water on a hard rock on which no vegetation or produce ever grows. This is because Muslims' hearts have become atrophied and encrusted with rust; their eyes have become bleary and can hardly distinguish between good and evil.

It has become evident that the various educational institutions in the Muslim world have miserably failed to produce the true, balanced Muslim individual. Universities which have been set up in Muslim countries on the lines of Western models do not see it as part of their task to prepare and produce Muslim scholars in all branches of knowledge so that they can Islamize the various disciplines at their disposal. Instead, they see their task as preparing graduates infatuated with the arts and sciences of the West. How quickly do such graduates turn their backs on the essential beliefs of Islam and its goals and objectives for life! These universities produce generations whose sense of belonging to Islam is weak, whose thinking is confused, and who are unable to use their knowledge in the service of the Muslim Ummah.

Educational institutions which are regarded as Islamic—such as al Azhar and other universities, colleges, and institutes patterned along similar lines, have achieved a limited success for the benefit of the Ummah. They have managed to produce some excellent specialists in some sciences of the Sharī'ah, but they have failed to provide the Ummah with able and innovative Muslim scholars and thinkers capable of presenting Islam as a holistic system with distinctive goals and objectives. Such scholars have not been able to confront contemporary challenges and overcome them. In the process, Islamic thought has atrophied and has failed to shape the thinking of Muslims and the direction of their lives. As a result, Muslim minds and hearts have remained wide open to the infiltration of all kinds of ideas which seek to subvert Islam. Muslims have become incapable of dealing with the problems facing them in politics, economics, social organization, and other fields. They have been content merely to transmit and imitate what others are thinking and doing.

This blind adoption of alien ideas and practices has created disagreement and dissension among various sections of the Ummah. These disagreements have mostly been resolved in the interests of

Western-minded groups who are culturally in thrall to the West. Instead of unifying their ranks and working together to face these threats and challenges, the devout Muslims unfortunately have become engaged in wrangling over controversial issues. This is mainly because of intellectual confusion and failure to distinguish between the parts and the whole, and between the ultimate purposes of the law and its underlying principles.

We are in desperate need of sound and vigorous Islamic thought which is built on an understanding of the spirit of Islam, its ultimate purposes, its overall principles, and the hierarchy of its laws derived from its great original sources—the Qur'an and the Sunnah. We also need to study the legacy and the methodology of our righteous forbears as they studied and acted upon these original sources in the early illustrious centuries. This will enable us to achieve a clear and complete perception that Islam is the only path for the salvation of the Muslim Ummah and that it contains the ideal solution for all its problems. This clear perception will rally the Ummah around the fundamentals of Islamic thought and will steer it away from evil intrigues and manipulations.

When the Ummah is thus firmly and correctly established and is able to identify its wounds, ailments, and the source of its malady, the steps which must be taken to arrive at the required cure and to realize the desired goal will undoubtedly become clear. That is well within its reach.

Chapter Ten

The Way Forward

It is important for the Muslims to realize that although God Almighty has made the Qur'an "easy to remember" and provided us with abundant sources for studying the Sunnah of the noble Prophet, individual initiatives to derive laws from these sources are fraught with difficulties and must be approached with caution.

The task requires adequate preparation in addition to a number of skills which the specialists in this field have detailed. It requires, for example, a knowledge of the principles and processes of deduction; an excellent command of the Arabic language and its stylistic features; and a knowledge of the sciences of the Qur'an and the Sunnah. In further detail, it involves, for example, a knowledge of "abrogation"–how one verse of the Qur'an supersedes another; of the general and the specific, identifying the general statement which can be construed as referring to something specific; identifying texts with an absolute application on the one hand and others with a restricted application, and several other factors and principles. Any judgment which a Muslim issues without a full knowledge and grasp of these requirements is no more than wishful thinking, guesswork, or a rough assessment arrived at without guidance or true knowledge. Whoever attempts to make a judgment in such a haphazard manner embarks on a perilous course and may even, God forbid, do himself a great injustice. The noble Prophet has said in this respect: "Whoever interprets the Qur'an without knowledge must take his seat in hell-fire."[1]

The type of knowledge required for interpreting the Qur'an and making judgments is not acquired through reading one or two books. It requires precise methodological study such as would provide the research-

---

1. Transmitted by al Tirmiḍhī with a sound *isnād* through Ibn 'Abbās.

er with the tools that will enable him to delve into the field of Islamic thought and Islamic disciplines. To be profitable, this kind of study must depend on exhaustive research conducted under the guidance of someone who has the necessary knowledge and the critical insight and who is motivated by a deep consciousness of God and the desire to seek only His reward.

It should be pointed out that the Sharī'ah has been revealed to bring happiness and prosperity to humanity in this life and in the hereafter. It seeks to realize the best interests of human beings in harmony with the mental capacities with which God has endowed them, thus honoring them over the rest of His creatures. The Sharī'ah, all-embracing and merciful as it is, does not include any matter which is unbearable for the human being. The Almighty says: "He has laid no hardship on you in [anything that pertains to] religion" (22: 78).

God has made it easy for His servants to live and function in harmony with His religion and in an atmosphere of spontaneous love, not through force or coercion: "God desires that you shall have ease, and does not desire you to suffer hardship" (2: 185), and "God wants to lighten your burdens" for God knows that "man has been created weak" (4: 28).

As stated above, all the laws of the Sharī'ah are for the welfare of human beings as servants of God. They are there to bring advantages to mankind and there is, of course, no benefit to God in them since God Almighty is "free from all wants, worthy of all praise." It is therefore imperative to understand the various parts of the Sharī'ah in the light of the totality and ultimate purposes of the law. Whoever does not have a grasp of the overall implications and purposes of the Sharī'ah and does not understand its basic principles could never deal adequately with the subsidiary branches (*furū'*) and details of the law adequately and in their proper context. Ibn Burhān[2] says:

> Divine laws are policies through which God regulates the affairs of His servants. The way of dealing with people in this regard varies according to the differences in time. Each period of time requires a type of regulation which caters to the general welfare specific to that time. In the same way, each nation

2. Aḥmad ibn 'Alī ibn Burhān al Baghdādī (d. 518 AH) was a well-known expert in jurisprudence and wrote several books on the subject. He was a Ḥanbalī but later followed Imām al Shāfi'ī.

has a type of regulation which is in its general interest, even though it may result in vitiating rights when applied to others.[3]

There is a consensus among Muslim scholars that the laws of the Sharī'ah – all of them – have as their underlying cause the realization of the public welfare (*maṣlaḥah*) and that it is precisely for this reason that they were prescribed. This is the case whether these laws are explicitly expressed in the original texts or derived from these texts. If there are points or areas on which there is no explicit divine guidance, we remain convinced that this is due to some wisdom known to God alone. As a consequence of this, many of the laws formulated on the basis of ijtihād change with the passing of time. These laws may also vary according to the differences between individuals in proportion to their capacities and circumstances.

At the same time, we should realize that the explicit texts of the Qur'an and that part of the Sunnah which is transmitted by several continuous chains (*mutawātir*) of narrators are categorically authentic. There is also a part of the Sunnah, such as a ḥadīth transmitted by only a single narrator, whose authenticity is not fully established. The intended meaning of a given text might be explicit or it might be inferred. A knowledge of all such matters has a direct bearing on the way in which a text is understood, on the process of *istinbāṭ*, and on ijtihād. No one has the right to reject an interpretation of a text advanced by others as long as the interpretation can be sustained by the text and is not in conflict with other legal texts. Most of the laws pertaining to subsidiary and practical matters are of the type that can be verified by logical processes, and this is part of the mercy of God to His servants which allows adequate scope for the exercise of analytical thought and judgment.

Since the Wise Lawgiver has made matters easy for people and has taken their welfare into consideration, it is unbecoming of anyone to accuse someone who differs with him on these matters of unbelief (*kufr*), corruption (*fisq*), or innovation (*bid'ah*). On the contrary, he should try to seek justification for the one who differs with him so as to strengthen the bond of affection between them and secure mutual respect, love, and brotherhood.

---

3. *Al Wuṣūl ilā al Uṣūl* (Getting to the Principles), manuscript.

Brotherhood and Solidarity

One of the most important responsibilities which all Muslims should be aware of is the duty to preserve the brotherhood and the solidarity of Muslims. Part of this duty is to scrupulously avoid anything that would corrupt or weaken these bonds. Preserving brotherhood is an important form of worship through which we can achieve nearness to God and overcome all the obstacles to a renewal of Muslim life. It is sufficient to recall that the noble Prophet aroused in us an abhorrence of disunity by sanctioning the most severe punishment for the one who deliberately splits from the community (*jamā'ah*). For this reason, any tendency to forsake Islamic brotherhood or be inunconcerned about it because of any difference of opinion is something which no Muslim is allowed to do. Moreover, he should be perceptive enough not to fall into the trap of dissension set by the enemies of Islam. This is especially so in our times, as many hostile forces and nations are pitted against us, seeking to stifle the sparks of faith which are being kindled anew in the hearts of the believers. With their wanton hands they seek to grind the tender shoots of the Islamic awakening into the dust.

Brotherhood for the sake of God and the unity of hearts among Muslims is high on the list of obligations incumbent on Muslims. It is close in importance to the duty of affirming the oneness of God (*tawḥīd*). There are also different levels of prohibitions, and causing damage to Muslim brotherhood also comes at the top of grave prohibitions. This is why the righteous scholars of old, when confronted with a controversial issue, often opted for the merely acceptable rather than the clearly preferable in order to preserve unity and leave no room for strife and dissension. In this spirit, they would forsake what in their view was recommended (*mandūb*) and just do what was allowed (*jā'iz*).

We have seen the deep respect and consideration which the early Muslims had for one another and their commitment to the unity and brotherhood of Muslims. No one should jump to the conclusion, however, that our keenness to preserve the brotherhood and solidarity of Muslims implies any negligence of the fundamental Islamic beliefs which are not open to any speculation or compromise. The determination to confront the enemies of the Ummah will prevent us from joining hands with those who do not have any affinity with Islam. The controversial issues which should not cause any disunity among us are those which have already been recognized by the early scholars. They dealt with these issues in the most proper and admirable manner.

It is common knowledge that the Sharī'ah has classified many of the acts of worship into what is preferable, optional, and permissible. These are all acceptable categories to God, but they differ in grade. Many of the compulsory and obligatory duties have several aspects which fall into the above three categories. It is possible to perform an act of worship relying on what is most preferable according to the Sharī'ah, and it will be justly rewarded. For example, performing an obligatory ṣalāh right at the beginning of its appointed time, performing it in congregation, and in addition performing the acts recommended according to the Sunnah is the most preferable course. Then again, one has the option to perform the same act of ṣalāh later in the time allowed, and this will fall under the second category of the optional. The third category is the permissible and this involves doing the bare minimum.

Ideals and Realities

According to a tradition: "The good deeds of the righteous, coming in later times, would have been considered demerits in the eyes of the early devout Companions."

In the light of the above saying, it would be safe to say that he who expects all people, irrespective of their circumstances and individual abilities, to realize the ideal vision of Islam is setting a goal which is not easy to attain. This points to a clear recognition of the fact that human abilities and actual efforts and energies expended vary from one individual to another. This is why there are various levels of worship and obedience, and these will be reflected in the varying levels of the believers in paradise.

In his commentary[4] on the Qur'an, Ibn Jarīr al Ṭabarī relates that some people met 'Abd Allāh (the son of 'Umar ibn al Khaṭṭāb) in Egypt and said to him: "We see teachings of the Qur'an which are adhered to by some and not by others. We want to meet the *Amīr al Mu'minīn* ('Umar Ibn al Khaṭṭāb) to question him about these matters." They went with him to 'Umar, may God be pleased with him. 'Abd Allāh told his father why they had come and so they were invited to meet him. When they were gathered, 'Umar looked at the nearest man to him and asked:

> "Tell me truly, by God and by the right of Islam over you, have you read the entire Qur'an?"

---

4. Al Ṭabarī, *Tafsīr*, 5/29.

> "Yes," replied the man.
>
> "Have you acted upon all of it as it affects you yourself?"
>
> "O Lord, no," replied the man.
>
> "Have you strictly followed the Qur'an in all that you see? Have you followed it in what you say? Have you followed it wherever your steps take you?"

'Umar then put the same questions to everyone in the audience. When he came to the last person he said:

> "May the mother of 'Umar lose her son! Do you [now expect me to] place an imposition on people to adhere to the entire Book of God? Our Lord and Sustainer certainly knew that we have failings," and he recited the following verse of the Qur'an: "If you shun the great sins which you have been forbidden to do, We shall efface your failings and cause you to enter [upon your afterlife] in a state of glory" (4: 31).

'Umar then asked whether the people of Egypt knew of their coming to make this complaint. Fortunately for them, they said: "No," as 'Umar threatened: "If they had known, I would have made an example out of you."

There is a profound lesson which 'Umar, may God be pleased with him, clarified in this incident. It is that the ideal vision which the Qur'an holds out for the Muslim is a model which he must try to realize or attain. Whenever he falls short of this model—as is inevitable—he should realize that God's mercy is indeed vast. When he avoids the major sins at least, he is assuredly on the way to attaining abundant good—if God wills. He has the obligation, however, to constantly strive towards the ideal vision and never to be content with the minimum standard.

Hopefully, a knowledge and understanding of the causes of difference of opinion among the early jurists and the context in which they occurred will assist us to reduce the causes of disagreement at present and enable us to develop and maintain the beautiful ethics and manners of dealing with them.

When the early scholars differed, they did so for objective reasons. They were all *mujtahidūn*, qualified and able to engage in analytical thought and make independent judgments. Each one of them was engaged in a rigorous search for truth, and it made no difference to anyone if the truth about any issue was discovered by someone else.

To help Muslims develop and stick to the ethics and proper norms (*adab*) of dealing with differences, it is imperative that they should be fully aware of the enormous dangers and threats as well as the malicious strategies which are constantly being engineered by the enemies of Islam to eliminate those who are in the vanguard of the Islamic awakening and *da'wah*. These strategies are targeted against all who strive for Islam irrespective of their schools of thought or any differences in their orientation. In this situation, any disagreement among Muslims, any attempt to perpetuate disagreements, or any flouting of the norms of proper behavior amounts to subversion of the objectives of the Ummah and is a crime which cannot be justified or excused.

Over and above all this, it is imperative that we maintain a deep consciousness of God (*taqwā*), both secretly and openly, and seek His pleasure in times of both agreement and disagreement. We need to have the determination to deepen our understanding of Islam, free from personal whims and negative influences. We need to be aware of how these negative influences work and how they ensnare us.

The Ummah has suffered enough. Now is the time for us to come to our senses and steadfastly follow the right course in the light of the Qur'an and the Sunnah. We entertain the hope that God Almighty, through the efforts of the righteous Muslims of this generation, will rescue this Ummah and lead it to the shores of safety and security after centuries of perilous wandering and error.

We ask God Almighty to teach us what is beneficial to us, to make us benefit from what He has taught us, and to increase our knowledge. May He unite us in the pursuit of truth, guide us to the right path, and crown all our actions with success. May He guard us against the evils of our thoughts and actions. May He protect us from the folly of "breaking into shreds the yarn which was once tightly spun and strong." In Him we seek refuge and on His might we depend. All praise and thanks are due to God, the Lord and Sustainer of all the worlds.

Glossary

Adab: (plural: *ādāb*). Refinement, ethical norms, and standards of behavior. Connotes discipline, proper etiquette, manners, and training. Refers in general to the discipline that comes from recognizing one's proper place in relation to one's self and others. It also refers to the proper etiquette or manner of carrying out particular actions. Loss of *ādāb* implies loss of discipline and a failure to act with justice.

'Ādah: Custom, practice. A local custom which is not in conflict with the Qur'an or the Sunnah (q.v.) is admissible as part of Islamic law.

'Adl: Justice, equilibrium.

Ahādīth: (singular: ḥadīth). The verbalized form of a tradition of the Prophet, peace be on him, constitutive of his Sunnah. A ḥadīth narrative is divided into two parts: the *isnād* (chain of transmission) and the *matn* (content of the narrative).

Ahl al Bayt: Literally, people of the house. Refers to the family and relations of the noble Prophet who were Muslims.

Ahl al Dhikr: Literally, people of remembrance. Refers to true scholars whose knowledge springs from and is steeped in the remembrance of God.

Ahl al Ḥadīth: Literally, people of ḥadīth. Refers to scholars who rely on authenticated sayings of the Prophet and who are wary of using independent reasoning (*ra'ī*) in making juristic judgments. Used in contradistinction to *ahl al ra'ī* (q.v. under *ra'ī*).

A'immah: See imam.

Ahl al Sunnah: Literally, people of the Sunnah. Refers to the vast majority of Muslims who follow the Sunnah (q.v) of the Prophet and the precedents of his rightly-guided successors. Used in contradistinction to the Shī'ah (q.v.) who believed that 'Alī, the Prophet's cousin and son-in-law, should have been his immediate successor. *Ahl al Sunnah wa al Jamā'ah*—the community united behind the Sunnah of the Prophet.

'Ālim: (plural: 'ulamā'): One who knows, a scholar, a scientist. Commonly used for someone who has a thorough knowledge of Islam and its sources, the Qur'an and the Sunnah. An important characteristic of an *'ālim*, according to the Qur'an, is that he is deeply conscious of God and stands in awe of Him.

Amīr al Mu'minīn: Literally, Commander of the Believers. The title was first given to any commander of a military mission but was later used specifically for the head of the Muslim state, the *khalīfah*.

'Āmm, al: The 'general' as opposed to the 'particular' (*al khāṣṣ*). Terms used by jurists in the complex matter of extracting laws from statements composed as codal propositions. Islamic scholarship called 'general' (*al 'āmm*) the term which comprehends a plurality, and distinguished two varieties of it —generality in the term itself and generality in the meanings to which the term may refer.

Anṣār: Literally, Helpers. Name given collectively to the Muslims native to Madinah during the time of the Prophet who pledged to support and defend him.

'Aqīdah: Belief; the substance of a belief.

Asbāb al Nuzūl: The causes or the circumstances and events surrounding a particular revelation of the Qur'an. Knowledge of the *asbāb al nuzūl* helps provide an understanding of the original context and intent of a particular revelation. This knowledge is necessary for determining the *ratio legis* of a ruling and whether, for example, the meaning of the revelation is of a specific or of general application.

Aṣl: (plural: *uṣūl*). Root, origin, source; principle.

Athar: Literally, impact, trace, vestige; deeds and precedents of the Companions of the Prophet.

Āyah: (plural: *āyāt*). Literally, sign, indication, message; an aspect of God's creation; a section of the Qur'anic text often referred to as a 'verse.'

Basmalah: The formula – *Bismillāh al Raḥmān al Raḥīm* – In the name of God, most Gracious, most Merciful.

Bāṭil: Null and void.

Baṭinīyah: (From *bāṭin* meaning hidden or esoteric). A sect of Sufis who sought alleged esoteric meanings behind the words of the Qur'an through allegorical interpretation. They also searched for a living infallible leader and had recourse to Greek Pythagorean theories.

Bayān: Exposition, explanation, clarification.

Bid'ah: Innovation. In contradistinction to the Sunnah. Refers to any action or belief which has no precedent in or has no continuity with the Sunnah. Any innovation introduced into the established practice of the noble Prophet, particularly relating to acts of worship, is regarded as erroneous according to his saying: "Every innovation (*bid'ah*) is an error (*ḍalālah*)."

Dalīl: (plural: *adillah*). Proof, indication, evidence. Every ruling or judgment needs to be substantiated by the appropriate *dalīl* in the first instance from the Qur'an and the Sunnah.

Da'wah: Invitation; call. Refers to the duty of Muslims to invite or call others to return to the straight and natural path of Islam or submission to God. This, according to the Qur'an, has to be done with wisdom and beautiful advice. The 'most excellent speech' is that of a person who calls others to God. *Da'wah* is addressed to both Muslims and non-Muslims.

Dīyah: Compensation.

Faqīh: (plural: *fuqahā'*). Literally, one who has a deep understanding of Islam, its laws, and jurisprudence; a jurist.

Fātiḥah, al: Literally, the Opening. The opening chapter of the Qur'an.

Far': (plural: *furū'*). Literally, branch, subdivision. A subsidiary law; a new case (in the context of *qiyās* (q.v.)).

Fatwā: (plural: *fatāwā*). Juridical verdict, legal opinion.

Fiqh: Literally, understanding. The legal science founded mainly on rules and principles developed by human reasoning (ijtihād) and the body of knowledge so derived. Fiqh may therefore vary from one jurist or school of thought to another. The term "fiqh" is sometimes used synonymously with Sharī'ah (q.v.). However, while fiqh is to a large extent the product of human endeavor, the Sharī'ah is closely related to divine revelation and knowledge which is only obtained from the Qur'an and the Sunnah.

Fitnah: Any affliction which may cause man to go astray and to lose his faith in spiritual values; test, trial, confusion, civil war, oppression.

Ghayb, al: That which is beyond the reach of human perception.

Ghusl: A bath performed in a prescribed manner and which is necessary to ensure purification after certain actions, for example, sexual intercourse, seminal emissions, menstruation.

Ḥadīth: see *aḥādīth* above.

Ḥadīth Ḍa'īf: Weak ḥadīth. One of the three main categories of ḥadīth in contradistinction to *ṣaḥīḥ* (authentic) and *ḥasan* (good) ḥadīth. A ḥadīth is weak owing to a weakness that exists in its chain of narrators or in its textual content. There are several varieties of weak ḥadīth.

Ḥadīth Marfū': Literally, an 'elevated' ḥadīth. Refers to a *ḥadīth mursal* (q.v.) which is consistent with the precedent of the Companions and which is 'elevated' and attributed to the Prophet.

Ḥadīth Mashhūr: A 'well-known' ḥadīth; a ḥadīth which is originally reported by one, two, or more Companions from the Prophet or from another Companion, but has later become well-known and transmitted by an indefinite number of people during the first and second generation of Muslims.

Ḥadīth Munqaṭi': A ḥadīth with part of its *isnād* missing. Also referred to as ḥadīth *mursal*.

Ḥadīth Mursal: A ḥadīth which a person from the second generation of Muslims (*Tābi'ūn*) has directly attributed to the Prophet without mentioning the last link, namely the Companion, who might have narrated it from the Prophet. More generally, a ḥadīth with part of its *isnād* missing.

Ḥadīth Mutawātir: Literally 'continuously recurrent' ḥadīth. A ḥadīth is classified as *mutawātir* only when it is reported by a very large number of people of proven reliability in such a way as to preclude any possibility of them all agreeing to perpetuate a falsehood. According to the majority of scholars, the authority of a *mutawātir* ḥadīth is equivalent to that of the Qur'an.

Ḥad īth Ṣaḥīḥ: Authentic ḥadīth. A ḥadīth is classified as *ṣaḥīḥ* when its narrators are all reliable and trustworthy, when its *isnād* is continuous and goes right back to the Prophet, and when the narration is free from any obvious or subtle defects.

Hawā: (plural: *ahwā'*). Vain or egotistical desire; individual passion; impulsiveness. Following one's own desires is described in the Qur'an as taking these desires as your 'god' or object of worship. Following *hawā* leads to arrogance and destruction and is contrasted with following the Sharī'ah which is designed to discipline and lead man to fulfillment and happiness.

Hijrah: Migration. The act of leaving a place to seek sanctuary of freedom or worship in another or for any other purpose. Also the act of leaving a bad practice in order to adopt a righteous way of life. Specifically, the hijrah refers to the Prophet's journey from Makkah to Madinah in the month of Rabī' al Awwal in the twelfth year of his mission, corresponding to June 622 AC. The Islamic calendar begins from this event (AH)

Hijrī: Pertaining to the hijrah.

Ḥīlah: Legal stratagem.

Ḥudaybīyah: A plain to the west of Makkah where a truce was concluded between the Prophet and the Quraysh in 6 AH.

Ḥudūd: (singular: *ḥadd*). Literally, limits; the specific punishments assigned by the Qur'an and the Sunnah for particular crimes—intoxication, theft, rebellion, adultery and fornication, false accusation of adultery, and apostasy. These crimes involve transgressing the limits of acceptable behavior.

Ḥujjīyah: Producing the necessary proof or authority to validate a rule or concept.

'Ibārat al Naṣṣ: Explicit meaning of a given text which is borne out by its words.

Ijmā': Consensus of opinion. Usually defined as the unanimous agreement of the *mujtahidūn* of any period following the demise of the Prophet Muḥammad on any matter. As such, it is described as collective ijtihād.

Ijtihād: Literally, striving and self-exertion; independent reasoning; analytical thought. Ijtihād may involve the interpretation of the source materials, inference of rules from them, or giving a legal verdict or decision on any issue on which there is no specific guidance in the Qur'an and the Sunnah.

Ikhtilāf: Difference of opinion; disagreement; dispute; controversy.

'Illah: (plural: *'ilal*). Effective cause or *ratio legis* of a particular ruling.

Imam: (plural: *a'immah*). Leader. May refer to the leader of congregational ṣalāh, to a leading and reputable scholar, or to the head of the Muslim state.

Isnād: Chain of narrators of a ḥadīth.

Istiḥsān: Juristic preference—the abandonment of one legal ruling for another which is considered better or more appropriate to a given circumstance.

Istinbāṭ: Inference. Deducing a somewhat hidden meaning from a given text. The process of extracting laws.

Istiṣḥāb: Presumption of continuity, or presuming continuation of the *status quo ante*. For example, *istiṣḥāb* requires that once a contract of sale, or of marriage, is concluded it is presumed to remain in force until there is a change established by evidence.

Jadal: Dialectics, wrangling, disputation.

Jamā'ah: Group, congregation, community.

Jā'iz: That which is allowed or permissible. As a rule, everything that is not prohibited is allowed.

Jihad: Literally, striving. Any earnest striving in the way of God, involving either personal effort, material resources, or arms for righteousness and against evil, wrongdoing and oppression. Where it involves armed struggle, it must be for the defense of the Muslim community or a just war to protect even non-Muslims from evil, oppression, and tyranny.

Junub: Impure. A person is considered to be in a state of impurity, for example, after sexual intercourse and seminal emissions. A person in such a state is normally required to perform *ghusl* (q.v.) before performing acts of worship like ṣalāh.

Kalām: Literally, 'words' or 'speech,' and referring to oration. The name applied to the discipline of philosophy and theology concerned specifically with the nature of faith, determinism and freedom, and the nature of the divine attributes.

Khabar al Wāḥid: A solitary ḥadīth reported by a single person from the Prophet. Also called *ḥadīth Āḥād. Khabar* means news or report.

Khalīfah: (plural: *khulafā'*). Steward, vicegerent; successor. Man is referred to as the *khalīfah* or steward of God on earth. The word *khalīfah* was used after the death of the noble Prophet Muḥammad to refer to his successor, Abū Bakr, as head of the Muslim community. Later it came to be accepted as the designation for the head of the Muslim state. Anglicized as caliph.

Khamar: Intoxicant: wine.

Khāṣṣ: The particular as opposed to the general (*'āmm*).

Khawārij: Seceders. Name given to a group of the followers of the *khalīfah* 'Alī who opposed his decision to agree to arbitration in the conflict with Mū'āwiyah in 38 AH/659 AC. Later on, this group recognized as legitimate only the first two caliphs. Abū Bakr and 'Umar. Theologically, they considered the sinner as a *kāfir*, an outlaw or apostate, whom it is legitimate and religiously imperative to fight.

Khilāf: Controversy, dispute, discord.

Khilāfah: Stewardship, vicegerency; successorship. Office of the head of the Muslim state. Also the designation of the political system of the Muslim state after the noble Prophet.

Khuṭbah: Sermon, oration, or *ex tempore* speech.

Kufr: Ingratitude to God and manifest disbelief in Him and His religion.

Madhhab: (plural: *madhāhib*). Literally, way of going. School of thought.

Mandūb: Recommended.

Maṣlaḥah: (plural: *maṣālih*). Considerations of public interest. It is generally held that the principal objective of the Sharī'ah and all its commandments is to realize the genuine *maṣlaḥah* or benefit of the people.

Maṣlaḥah al Mursalah, al: (plural: *al maṣāliḥ al mursalah*). A consideration which is proper and harmonious with the objectives of the Lawgiver; it secures a benefit or prevents a harm, but the Sharī'ah provides no in dication as to its validity or otherwise. For example, the Companions decided to issue currency, to establish prisons, and to impose a tax on agricultural lands despite the fact that no textual authority could be found for these measures.

Mujtahid: (plural: *Mujtahidūn*). One who exercises ijtihād (q.v.).

Muqallid: (plural: *Mugallidūn*). One who follows or imitates another, often blindly and unquestioningly.

Murji'ah: Deferrers. Those who defer judgment of the sinner to God and the Day of Judgment.

Mushrik: (plural: *mushrikūn*). One who associates others in worship with God; a polytheist.

Mutashābihāt: Allegorical. Refers to verses (*āyāt*) of the Qur'an which are expressed in a figurative manner in contradistinction to *āyāt muḥkamāt* or verses which are clear in and by themselves.

Mu'tazilah: Group of rationalist thinkers who flourished from the middle of the second to the beginning of the fourth *hijrī* century.

Naskh: Abrogation of certain parts of the Qur'anic revelation by others. The principle is mentioned in the Qur'an: "None of Our revelations do We abrogate or cause to be forgotten, but We substitute something better or similar" (2: 106).

Nāsikh: (active participle). Refers to the passage which abrogates or supersedes the part which is abrogated. The abrogated passage is called *mansūkh* (passive participle).

Naṣṣ: (plural: *nuṣūṣ*). Text. A clear textual ruling or injunction from the Qur'an and the Sunnah.

Qaṭ'ī: Definitive, unequivocal; free of speculative content.

Qiyās: Analogical deduction or reasoning. Recourse to analogy is only warranted if the solution of a new case cannot be found in the Qur'an and the Sunnah. Analogy then consists in extending a principle (*aṣl*) derived from the Qur'an and the Sunnah to the new case. Analogical deduction cannot operate independently of the *nuṣūṣ*.

Ra'i: Opinion, reason. *Ahl al Ra'ī*—scholars who employ independent reasoning to the solution of new problems, in contradistinction to scholars who confine themselves mainly to ḥadīth (*q.v. Ahl al ḥadīth*).

Sadd al Dharā'i': Literally, blocking the means. Implies blocking the means to an expected end or an evil which is likely to materialize if the means towards it is not obstructed. For example, illicit privacy between members of the opposite sex is blocked or made unlawful because

Ṣaḥābah: Companions of the Prophet.

Salaf: Forebears, predecessors, ancestors. *Al Salaf al Ṣāliḥ*—the righteous forebears—refers to the early generations of Muslims including the *Ṣaḥābah* and the *Tābi'ūn*.

Shahādah: Testimony, witness; the act of witnessing that there is no god but Allah and that Muḥammad is His prophet, servant, and messenger; the verbal content of this act; martyrdom.

Shiqāq: Discord, schism, breach.

Shī'ah: Literally, sect or party. The term Shī'ah is short for *Shī'at* 'Alī or Sect of 'Alī. They believed that 'Ali, the cousin and son-in-law of the Prophet, should have succeeded him after the Prophet' death.

Sunnah: Literally, a clear path or beaten track. Refers to whatever the Prophet said, did, agreed to, or condemned. The Sunnah is a source of the Sharī'ah and a legal proof next to the Qur'an. As a source of the Sharī'ah, the Sunnah may corroborate a ruling which originates in the Qur'an. Secondly, the Sunnah may consist of an explanation or clarification of the Qur'an. Thirdly, the Sunnah may also consist of rulings on which the Qur'an is silent.

Tābi'ūn: Literally, followers. The generation of Muslims immediately after the Companions (Ṣaḥābah).

Tafsīr: Commentary, exegesis of the Qur'an.

Taqlīd: Uncritical adoption or imitation of a particular scholar or school of thought (*madhhab*).

Taqwā: Consciousness of God.

Tawbah: Literally, returning. Repenting and seeking forgiveness for one's sins in order to return as close as possible to one's originally good and unsullied state.

Tawḥīd: Belief in or affirmation of the Oneness of God.

Ta'wīl: Interpretation or explanation. Sometimes used synonymously with *tafsīr*. Often used in the Qur'an in the sense of 'final meaning,' 'inner meaning' or 'real meaning' of a happening or statement or thing as distinct from its outward appearance. Absolute knowledge or what a thing or event implies rests with God alone—"none except God knows its final meaning—*ta'wīl*" (3: 7).

Tayammum: Symbolic ablution in place of *wuḍū'*, performed, for example, in the absence of water or in the case of illness.

'Ulamā': (singular: *'ālim*). See *'ālim* above.

Ummah: (plural: *umam*). Community, nation. Specifically, the community of believers or the universal Muslim community.

'Urf: Local custom which is 'recognizably' good. In the absence of anything to the contrary, derivation of the law from the common and approved mores of a people.

Uṣūl: (singular, *aṣl*). Principles, origins. *Uṣūl al fiqh*—principles of Islamic jurisprudence, philosophy of law; the methodology of deriving laws from the sources of Islam and of establishing their juristic and constitutional validity.

Waqf: (plural: *awqāf*). Charitable endowment or trust set up in perpetuity.

Wuḍū': Purification that must precede ṣalāh and such acts as the reading of the Qur'an.

Ẓāhir: Manifest, apparent, obvious. A word or phrase is described as *ẓāhir* when it has a clear meaning. It may still however be open to interpretation.

Zakāh: The compulsory 'purifying' tax on wealth which is one of the five 'pillars' of Islam. The word zakāh is derived from the word meaning purification, growth, and sweetening.

Ẓannī: Speculative, doubtful. Refers to a text which is open to interpretation as opposed to a text which is definitive, unequivocal (*qaṭ'ī*).

INDEX OF QUR'ANIC VERSES

INDEX OF HADITH TEXTS

GENERAL INDEX

A

'Abd Allāh ibn Aḥmad ibn Ḥanbal, 104
'Abd Allāh ibn al Mubārak, 103
'Abd Allāh ibn Ḥakam, 104
abrogation, 87, 127
Abū 'Ubaydah, 41
Abū al Dardā', 100
Abū Bakr, 32, 33, 36, 37, 39, 41, 42, 45, 65
Abū Dāwūd, 23
Abū Ḥanīfah, 59, 60, 66, 67, 69, 70, 71, 73, 75, 77, 92, 97, 98, 102, 103, 114, 116
Abū Hurayrah, 43
Abū Mūsā, 46, 47, 52, 64
Abū Nuwās, 114
Abū Thawr, 70
Abū Yūsuf, 71, 92
Abū Zar'ah, 101
'ādah, 88
Adam, 83, 100
adultery, 66
ahl al ra'y, 63, 70
'Ā'ishah, al Sayyidah, 39, 50, 52, 92
'Alī ibn Abū Tālib , 25, 38, 45, 46, 48, 49, 50, 51, 52, 53, 64, 65
'Alqamah, 60
'āmm, 72
'Ammār ibn Yāsir, 50, 64
'Amr ibn al 'Āṣ, 23, 51, 52
'Amr ibn Shu'ayb, 59
analogy, 66, 67, 72, 76, 77, 98
Anṣār, 38, 39, 40, 42, 57
'aqīdah, 79
Aqra' ibn Ḥābis, 32
Arabic language, 11, 12, 28, 121, 122, 127
asbāb al nuzūl, 27
aṣl, 75
Aswad, al, 59, 60
athar, 64
atheism, 16, 17
Awzā'ī, 'Abd al Raḥmān al, 59, 60, 69, 102

B

Badr, 49
Banū 'Abbās, 70
Banū Qurayẓah, 22
Basrah, 57, 61, 80, 106
Bātinīyah, 28
Battle of the Camel, 50
Battle of the Confederates, 21
beliefs, 17, 55, 130
bid'ah, 67, 129
bigotry, 106

C

camels, 58
chess, 114
Christianity, 16, 121
Christians, 4, 11
colonialism, 121
communism, 16, 122

Confederates, the Battle of the, 21

D
ḍa'īf, 76
da'wah, 41, 133
dalīl, 81, 88
Damascus, 61
Dāwūd ibn 'Alī al Iṣbahānī, 57, 106
Day of Judgment, 35
deduction, 82
democracy, 122
Dhāt al Salāsil, 23
Ḍirār ibn Damrah, 53, 54
divorce, 47
dīyah, 46, 58
drunkenness, 114

E
education, 121, 122
Egypt, 57, 93, 132
ethics, 8, 9, 13, 14
Europe, 121
evidence, 95

F
Faḍl ibn Mūsā, al, 103
faith, 2, 3, 8, 16, 55, 66, 111
fanaticism, 6, 33, 106
fasting, 66
fatāwā, 111
Fātiḥah, al, 17
fatwā, 29, 30
fiqh, 26, 27, 81
fitnah, 39
fuqahā', 55

G
ghayb, 27
Ghazzālī, al, 95, 96, 107, 110, 112
ghusl, 23
golden calf, 18

H
hadith, 74, 75, 76, 82, 85, 86, 87, 101, 102, 103, 105, 110, 117, 119
    marfū', 76
    mashhūr, 75
    munqaṭi', 74
    mursal, 75, 76, 77
    mutawātir, 129
Ḥammād, 59, 60
Hanafi school, 110, 111
Hārūn al Rashīd, 18, 19, 92
Ḥasan al Baṣrī, 58, 69
Hijaz, 62, 63, 70, 76, 82, 92, 93
ḥikmah, 40
Hishām ibn 'Urwah, 70
Ḥudaybīyah, 52
ḥudūd, 113
Ḥunayn, 57, 63
hypocrisy, 34

I
Iblīs, 66
Ibn 'Abbās, 24, 26, 36, 48, 49, 51, 85
Ibn 'Ajlān, 100
Ibn Abū Laylā, 99

J

K

U

'ulamā', 17, 26, 27, 28, 45, 63
'Umar ibn al Khaṭṭāb, 32, 33, 36, 37, 38, 39, 41, 43-48, 57, 58, 92, 131, 132
'Umar ibn 'Abd al 'Azīz, 63
'urf, 88
Usāmah, 29, 30
uṣūl, 69
uṣūl al fiqh, 88
'Uthmān ibn 'Affān, 55, 57, 61, 65, 80

W

waqf, 45, 114
war, 45
war prisoners, 45
Wāṣil ibn 'Aṭā', 5, 6
welfare, 107
witness, 95
women, 58
wuḍū', 17, 92, 113

Y

Yaḥyā ibn Ma'īn, 105
Yaḥyā ibn Sa'īd al Qaṭṭān, 58, 102, 104
Yaḥyā ibn Yaḥyā, 115
Yamāmah, 58
Yemen, 58

Z

ẓāhir, 22, 27
Ẓāhirī school, 77
zakah, 42, 43, 44, 109
Zayd ibn Thābit, 48, 49
Zubayr ibn al 'Awwām, 38
Ẓuhrī, Ibn Shihāb al, 59, 60, 62, 97

IIIT ENGLISH PUBLICATIONS

A. Islamization of Knowledge Series

- *The Islamic Theory of International Relations: New Directions for Islamic Methodology and Thought* (1407/1987) by 'AbdulḤamīd AbūSulaymān.
- *Islamization of Knowledge: General Principles and Work Plan*, 3rd edition (1409/1989). A German edition was published under the title *Das Einbringen des Islam in das Wissen* (1408/1988).
- *Toward Islamic Anthropology: Definitions, Dogma, and Directions* (1406/1986) by Akbar S. Aḥmad.
- *Toward Islamic English* (1406/1986) by Ismā'īl Rājī al Fārūqī. A German edition was published under the title: *Für ein Islamisches Deutsch* (1408/1988).
- *Modelling Interest-Free Economy: A Study in Microeconomics and Development* (1407/1987) by Muḥammad Anwar.
- *Islam: Source and Purpose of Knowledge*. Papers presented to the Second International Conference of Islamic Thought and the Islamization of Knowledge (1409/1988).
- *Toward Islamization of Disciplines*. Papers presented to the Third International Conference on Islamic Thought and the Islamization of Knowledge (1409/1988).
- *The Organization of the Islamic Conference: An Introduction to an Islamic Political Institution* (1408/1988) by 'Abdullāh al Aḥsan.
- *Proceedings of the Lunar Calendar Conference*. Papers presented to the Conference of the Lunar Calendar. Edited by Imād ad-Dean Ahmad (1408/1988).
- *Islamization of Attitudes and Practices in Science and Technology.* Papers presented to a special seminar on the same topic (1409/1989). Edited by M.A.K. Lodhi.
- *Where East Meets West: The West on the Agenda of the Islamic Revival* (1412/1992) by Mona Abul-Fadl.

- *Qur'anic Concept of Human Psyche.* Papers presented to a special seminar organizerd by IIIT Pakistan (1412/1992). Edited by Zafar Afaq Ansari.

- *Islam and the Economic Challenge* by M. Umer Chapra. Published jointly with the Islamic Foundation (U.K.) (1412/1992).

- *Resource Mobilization and Investment in an Islamic Economic Framework.* Papers presented to the 3rd International Islamic Economics Seminar (1412/1991). Edited by Zaidi Sattar.

B. Issues in Contemporary Islamic Thought Series

- *Islamic Thought and Culture.* Papers presented to the Islamic Studies Group of the American Academy of Religion (1402/1982). Edited by Ismā'īl Rājī al Fārūqī.

- *Trialogue of the Abrahamic Faiths*, 2nd edition (1406/1986). Papers presented to the Islamic Studies Group of the American Academy of Religion. Edited by Ismā'īl Rājī al Fārūqī.

- *Islamic Awakening: Between Rejection and Extremism* by Yūsuf al Qaraḍāwī. Published jointly with American Trust Publications. (new revised edition, 1412/1992).

- *Madīnan Society at the Time of the Prophet* (1411/1991) by Akram Ḍiyā' al 'Umarī,
    - Volume I: *Its Characteristics and Organization.*
    - Volume II: *The Jihad Against the Mushrikūn*

- *Tawḥīd: Its Implications for Thought and Life* (second edition, 1412/1992) by Ismā'īl Rājī al Fārūqī.

C. Research Monographs Series

- *Source Methodology in Islamic Jurisprudence: (Uṣūl al Fiqh Islāmī),* (third edition, 1413/1993) by Ṭāhā Jābir al 'Alwānī.

- *Islam and the Middle East: The Aesthetics of a Political Inquiry* (1411/1990) by Mona Abul-Fadl.

- *Sources of Scientific Knowledge: The Concept of Mountains in the Qur'an* (1411/1991) by Zaghloul R. El-Naggar.

D. Occasional Papers Series

- *Outlines of a Cultural Strategy* (1410/1989) by Ṭāhā Jābir al 'Alwānī. A French edition was published under the title *Pour une Stratégie Culturelle Islamique* (1411/1990), and a German edition was Published under the title *Entwurf Eines Alternativen Kulturplanes* (1413/1992).
- *Islamization of Knowledge: A Methodology* (1412/1991) by 'Imād al Dīn Khalil. A French edition was published under the title *Méthodologie Pour Islamisation du Savoir* (1412-1991).
- *The Qur'an and the Sunnah: The Time-Space Factor* (1412/1991) by Ṭāhā Jābir al 'Alwānī and 'Imād al Dīn Khalīl. A French edition was published under the title *Le Coran et La Sunna: Le Facteur Temps-Espace* (1412/1992).
- *Knowledge: An Islamic Perspective* (1412/1991) by Bakhtiar Ḥusain Siddiqui.
- *Islamization of Knowledge: A critical overview* (1413-1992) by Sayyed Vali Reza Nasr.
- *Ijtihad* (1413/1993) by Ṭāhā Jābir al Ālwānī

E. Human Development Series

- *Training Guide for Islamic Workers* by Hisham Altalib, (third revised edition 1413-1993). A Turkish and a Malay edition were published in (1412/1992).

F. Perspectives on Islamic Thought Series:

- *National Security and Development Strategy* (1412-1991) by Arshad Zaman.
- *Nationalism and Internationalism in Liberalism, Marxism and Islam* (1412/1991) by Tahir Amin.

Journals

- *American Journal of Islamic Social Sciences* (AJISS). A quarterly published jointly with the Association of Muslim Social Scientists (AMSS), U.S.A.
- *Muslim World Book Review* and *Index of Islamic Literature.* A quarterly published jointly with the Islamic Foundation (U.K.).

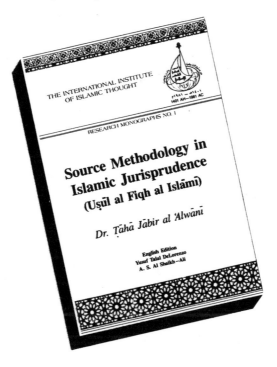

Distributors of IIIT Publications

Belgium Secompex, Bd. Mourice Lemonnier, 152
1000 Bruxelles Tel: (32-2) 512-4473 Fax: (32-2) 512-8710

Egypt IIIT Office, 26-B Al Jazirah al Wusṭa St., Zamalek, Cairo
Tel: (202) 340-9520 Fax: (202) 340-9520

France Libraire Essalam, 135 Boulevard de Ménilmontant
75011 Paris Tel: (33-1) 4338-1956 Fax: (33-1) 4357-4431

Holland Rachad Export, Le Van Swindenstr. 108 II
1093 Ck. Amsterdon Tel: (31-20) 693-3735 Fax: (31-20) 693-882x

India Genuine Publications & Media (Pvt.) Ltd., P.O. Box 9725
Jamia Nagar, New Delhi 110 025 Tel: (91-11) 630-989 Fax: (91-11) 684-1104

Jordan IIIT Office, P.O. Box 9489, Amman
Tel: (962-6) 639-992 Fax: (962-6) 611-420

Lebanon IIIT, c/o United Arab Bureau, P.O. Box 135788, Beirut
Tel: (961-1) 807-779 Fax: c/o (212) 478-1491

Morocco Dār al Amān for Publishing and Distribution,
4 Zangat al Ma'muniyah, Rabat Tel: (212-7) 723-276 Fax: (212-7) 723-276

Saudi Arabia International House for Islamic Books,
P.O. Box 55195, Riyadh 11534
Tel: (966-1) 1-465-0818 Fax: (966-1) 1-463-3489

United Arab Emirates Reading for All Bookshop, P.O. Box 11032 Dubai
Tel: (971-4) 663-903 Fax: (971-4) 690-084

United Kingdom

- Muslim Information Services, 233 Seven Sisters Rd.
London N4 2DA Tel: (44-71) 272-5170 Fax: (44-71) 272-3214
- The Islamic Foundation, Markfield Da'wah Centre, Rutby Lane
Markfield, Leicester LE6 ORN, U.K.
Tel: (44-530) 244-944/45 Fax: (44-530) 244-946

U.S.A.

- Islamic Book Service, 10900 W. Washington St.
Indianapolis, IN 46231 U.S.A. Tel.: (317) 839-9248 Fax: (317) 839-2511
- Al Sa'dāwi/United Arab Bureau, P.O. Box 4059, Alexandria, VA 22303 USA
Tel: (703) 329-6333 Fax: (703) 329-8052

To order IIIT Publications write to the above listed distributors or contact:
IIIT Department of Publications, P.O. Box 669 Herndon, VA 22070-4705
Tel: (703) 471-1133 Fax: (703) 471-3922